0

D1825481

A Fly on the Ward

Copyright © Michael K Chapman 2012

A Fly on the Ward: Introduction

Hospitals are seen by most as places of illness, disease and injury, and of course this is true. However there is a lighter side to being an inpatient in hospital, not much of one I will agree, but if one looks and listens, a definite sense of humour can be detected rippling around the wards, corridors and broom cupboards. Although most people have been to hospital at least once during their lives, many have never even set foot in one. Numerous individuals still look on hospitals with suspicion and distrust, viewing them as modern human abattoirs designed to reduce the growing mass of human population or venues of sombre concern. This is not true as hospitals can also be places of fun, friendship, love and hope. So for those who still believe doctors use sorcery and potions consisting of frog's eyes and newt's tails, things have progressed slightly over the years! Multitudes of ailments, coughs, sneezes and diseases are successfully treated and allow suffers to return to their lives with little more than the odd scar or malpractice suit. Hospitals heal, cure and restore health and well being to millions each and every day. So please belay any fears or trepidation, hospitals and the hordes of medical professionals that inhabit them are solely there to help and maintain our health and assist in our efforts to remain on this mortal Earth for as long as we can.

Hospitals are the modern world's greatest equalisers, people from all races, creeds, wealth, upbringing and status can find themselves in a hospital bed next to someone far removed from their own social standing in life. From a young boy fascinated by his fellow patient, who was a flight lieutenant in the Royal Air Force, to a struggling musician discovering a music producer in the same ward. The weirdest I have so far come across was being incarcerated in a bed next to a doctor! One always assumes doctors are above illness, disease or injury but even they are human and prone to all ails and mishaps that plague the human race. Hospitals treat the sick, that is their destiny and duty of course, but this does not mean they are only venues of sadness and despair. Many wonderful and miraculous recoveries also occur, and countless people leave hospital and continue to lead full and healthy lives. Others of course may not be so lucky and leave a medical establishment with ongoing diseases and injuries that cannot be mended by modern medicine. However even these poor souls frequently discover new friends or fellow sufferers that help to comfort them amidst their own troubles.

But by far the most common situation that arises in hospitals is that of humour. The human race is gifted with the ability to laugh and joke in otherwise serious situations. Every ward will have its joker or the kindly patient who takes it upon his/her self to aid those around them as best they can. From simply talking to a lonely and frightened fellow patient, to fetching and carrying for those who are bed bound. I have never been in a hospital where a humorous or strange event did not come to light at some point during my stay. Too much importance is placed on feeling sympathy, concern or even fear when one is admitted into hospital. This need not be the case as hospitals can be a place of human interaction, faith and friendship as well as medicine and care. So next time you feel the need to be carted off to your local medical hostelry, do not fear or quake because you may find people that will enrich your life in ways you never thought possible.

During my frequent visits I have had the pleasure of meeting some extraordinary people, patients, nurses and doctors, porters, cleaners and even the odd visitor. Many of these people have enriched my life in many different ways. From the caring and concerned nurses, to the cheerful and helpful porters; to the friendly cleaners, the entertaining fellow patients and even the occasional pleasant doctor. Not once have I encountered Messer's Burke & Hare, nor Dr Crippen nor Dr Jekyll, though some did make me wonder! All have stamped impressions on me throughout my frequent trips as an inpatient and some have left memories I will long cherish.

I mention my hospital history not for sympathy but as an explanation and a background for the stories told. I have had both good times and bad times but along the way I have met and known some wonderful people. It is the antics and activities of these people I am now relating, not as tales of woe and misfortune but inspiration, amusement, and the inner strength that helps guide us through times of illness or injury.

Not all my servitude as a patient resulted from illness although much of it did. No, some of my own antics often lead me to face the dreaded Accident and Emergency department of a local hospital. I am totally accident prone! My family and friends reach for a first aid kit whenever I reach for a power tool, saw or even pliers. It is not that I do not concentrate while working on a job, DIY or hobby, it's just that I concentrate too hard and forget what is happening in the environment around me.

For instance I once drilled right through my left hand after the battery on my cordless drill became discharged and I switched to my electric drill instead. I took no account of the differing power output between a battery drill and an electric power drill. Without thinking I offered up the power drill and bit to the area I was working on and failed to compensate for the difference in both speed and torque capabilities. Click, on came the drill, slip, off the work area it slid, ouch, right through the hand I was using to hold the work area still! This action of course concluded in yet another trip to hospital, as an outpatient this time. Much amusement echoed round the waiting room and the ward as staff, fellow patients, doctors and even the interested passerby laughed at my most stupid mistake! I still have the gore covered drill bit somewhere.

Other accidents which deny explanation include the ability to insert a pair of pointed nose pliers deep into my wrist, even though they were initially stored safely in my coat pocket. Or the time I managed to stab myself with a red hot welding rod. I unthinkingly attempted to alter its position in my hand by pushing it against my stomach! Or the time I fell of the stage where I was performing as a DJ, ripping my leg open along my shin. This one was more easily explained, I was drunk! I was so very drunk that at the time it all seemed hilarious, but not for long. My drunken hilarity resulted in numerous stitches and a ruined pair of jeans.

So not all of my hospitalisation has been down to ill health, but I will admit that the bulk of them have been. I have not had the healthiest of lives but I am not complaining, grumbling or crying 'Woe is me!' into my bedpan. I am attempting to portray some of the strength, wit, humour and determination ordinary people display when faced with an illness or injury serious enough to land them in a hospital bed. Beware though; some of the stories may also portray stupidity, rashness, confusion and anarchy, not to mention a frequent lack of intelligence or understanding. I am simply hoping to relate a few of the humorous, some sad and some utterly unimaginable stories and events that have befallen me during my hundreds of incarcerations as a hospital patient.

Simple stories are often the best, the shortest stories can be even better. For example, during the early hours of one morning in a hospital ward, a male patient nearing his allotted three score years and ten, stood quietly beside his bed. Both the duty nurse and I noticed this, the nurse was busy so decided to wait and see what he intended to do, I was just curious with nothing else to do and sleep eluded me. Some minutes passed and the patient didn't move. More time passed and still he hadn't moved apart from raising the back of his hand near to his face occasionally. After watching the patient intermittently for some time, the night nurse finally approached the patient with some concern and asked him if he was alright.

'I'm fine,' he declared as he once more raised his hand to his face momentarily.

'Why are you standing here? Shouldn't you be in bed and asleep?' the nurse asked quietly.

'I'm off to meet my wife soon,' he replied.

'Ah,' whispered the nurse, 'Is she coming to see you tomorrow?'

'No, I'm going to meet her in a minute or two,' stated the patient with yet another glance at his hand.

'OK, excuse me for asking, but how are you going to meet your wife in a minute or two? Is she coming here?'

'No, she's not coming here this time of night. I'm off to meet her.'

'I don't think so, I think you should be back in your bed and trying to get some sleep.' stated the nurse as kindly as possible.

'No I'm still waiting thank you.'

'What are you waiting for if your wife is not coming here?'

'I'm waiting for the bus.'

With a sign of resignation, the patient once again looked at his hand, looked back at the nurse and said, 'I'm trying to get the bus home, but I think it's late!'

Once more he raised his wrist up to his face, peered at it for a few seconds before lowering it again with a loud sigh.

He didn't have a watch on either!

If there is one thing I have noticed during all my hospital stays, is that most patients who make a lot of noise, who talk in their sleep or even to themselves, who undertake strange actions like waiting for a bus at the bottom of their bed, or wandering the ward aimlessly at night, all tend to make good recoveries, being discharged from the hospital within days. So I am not playing on the misfortunes of others, rather I am highlighting the wonderful way the human body repairs and heals itself, the fact that the route to recovery includes some hilarity is an added bonus. While each story has some truth in it, I have embellished most with events, words or actions that may only be true in my memories. Some storylines happened many years ago and so age may have altered these memories, either age or senility, but all these tales observed from a hospital bed are based, often loosely on real life events or situations.

Hopefully these stories will help belay these fears and superstitions, possibly some will create a laugh or two, but most importantly it is intended these stories will pacify those in terror of the medical profession and our hospitals.

Chapter One: A female visitor . . .

I awoke in the early hours of the morning with the definite feeling that something was wrong, different, something had awoken me that was not amongst the normal snores, farts, coughs, groans, shuffles to the toilet or nurses chatter. Quickly I opened my eyes and waited for them to adjust to the gloom of the room. At night in a hospital ward, it is never truly dark due to lights shining in from every internal and external orifice including the corridor, safety night lights in the ceiling, or bedside lamps left on as patients fall asleep while reading. The bright screens of monitors and the assorted machines that often accompany those who require constant observation also help keep the night darkness from full penetration.

After just a few moments I could see clearer and I peered about the room, automatically noting the bulge of each fellow ward patient on their individual beds. So it was not the moving of a ward mate that had disturbed me, maybe something was going on outside in the corridor? No all was quiet, not even the sound of nurses talking or clinking tea cups. OK thought I, it must be something closer. I began to shift in my bed, getting myself into a position from which to sit up and examine the area immediately around my bed space. As my legs straightened I felt something. It felt like someone was sitting on the bottom of my bed! I whipped my head round and with a sharp, un-polite exclamation I did discover there was a person sat calmly on my bed!

'Hello,' I said cautiously to the person's small back.

'Hello, are you OK?'

The person shifted position slightly and muttered softly in reply, 'I don't know where I am.'

Relief! The voice was that of an old lady and matched what I could distinguish from her body outline. Her voice sounded so sad, so pitiful and lost that I felt some reassurance, normally screaming for help would be my chosen course of action.

'You're in hospital love,' I said, 'you must have wandered out of your ward. What's your name?'

'I don't know where I am,' she replied, 'can you tell me where I am?'

Once again I repeated in a quiet and calm voice, 'You're in hospital love, you must be poorly and you're in hospital to get better.'

This seemed to calm her, but only for a moment before she again asked me where she was. By now I was growing concerned. What if she was very ill and needed help? What if she was contagious? I certainly had enough health problems of my own without the added risk of catching someone else's choice disease. OK so what do I do? I felt sure if I got out of bed and searched for a nurse, the little old lady would wander off somewhere and it may be hours before she was found again. I also feared she may stumble onto one of the other patient's beds and scare the living daylights out of both of them! All the other male patients in my bay were on the elderly side and any shock or fright at this hour of night could cause unfortunate repercussions, in several disconcerting ways. I had fleeting visions of five elderly men and one elderly woman screaming in panic, heart attacks, strokes, sudden bowel movements, faints or flight turning the ward in to a scene perfect for a `Carry On film´!

As my mind raced through the possible solutions, I continued to try and placate the women, she still had not moved, not even turned to look at me, she just kept staring at the wall in front of her.

'No need to worry love, you're in hospital being looked after.'

Silence.

'Are you alright love?' I continued with some desperation creeping into my voice.

There was a small shuffle in position but still no reply from the old lady.

'What's your name love?' I questioned again, 'Can I help?'

Finally a reply, 'I don't know where I am,' she whispered, 'can you tell me how to get home please?'

Hell, now I began to panic, was she real or was I seeing a ghost? Was I actually still asleep and dreaming? No, I didn't think so, I'm very sure I would be dreaming of someone more appealing than a mysterious little old lady. Quickly I glanced about the ward, hoping someone had woken up and noticed my dilemma. Nothing, all the bulges were still and the snores, farts, coughs and groans were still providing an audio back drop to the strange scene unfolding on my bed. Panic struck fully at last. As fast but as calmly as I could I reached for the nurse call button, no easy task as I had no idea where it was. Even when ill I strive to be independent, never asking for help if possible and always trying not to bother the already very busy nurses. So first I had to manoeuvre slowly about my bed area searching for the nurse call button. Found it! Frantically I pressed the large orange button that would alert the nurses to my call, eventually. I say this not in disrespect to the nurses but rather in awareness of the tough job they do. I may have rung my bell to gain attention but it still relied on what the nurses were doing elsewhere at that time. Another patient may be in serious need of attention or they may already be involved in one of the numerous tasks they have to complete during the course of their shift. So I pressed my call button and prepared to wait.

Luckily Edward, the male staff nurse came into the ward soon after, he glanced quickly round the room peering into the dimness for an indication of who was seeking assistance. Of course as I hardly ever rang my bell, I was the very last patient he looked at. As urgently as I could while attempting not to appear panicked, I waved him over to my bed. At first he didn't see my quiet guest, sat on the bottom of my bed in the gloom.

'What's up?' he asked, surprise showing on his face as he registered it was I who pressed the call button.

Without saying a word I pointed to the bottom of my bed, he looked, he saw, he nearly swore, and then he sprang into action. In a moment he identified the old woman as a patient from the female bay just along the ward corridor. She must have quietly wandered out from her bed, out of her room, along the short corridor and into mine while the night staff were preoccupied with other patients. This in itself was not uncommon nor in most cases is it a serious issue, many patients sleep poorly at night, many wander, many just leave their beds to stretch their legs, almost all take nightly trips to the toilet, and some even go in search of a hot drink that can be obtained from the nurses if sleep is elusive. Patients moving along the corridors between the ward bays cause little concern unless they are too unsteady on their feet, sleep walking or in a drugged and unaware state of mind, or drunk if a Friday or Saturday night!

At this point I must point out that the layout of this particular hospital consists of a large ward which contains four bays, each bay beds five or six patients, two bays for women, two bays for men and four, I think, individual side rooms for those who are extremely ill or contagious in some way. A corridor links all the bays, nurses' station, the side rooms, store rooms, toilets and washrooms together in one single unit. Patients often stroll along their half of the link corridor, men courteously keeping to the area between the two male bays and the women doing the same in their half of the corridor, and rarely do the two ever meet.

As soon as Edward had identified the woman, he moved to her, gently took hold of her arm and with a soft voice, quietly helped her to her feet and led her off to her own room. The old lady was still repeating the statement that she did not know where she was, in her sad voice as she shuffled out of my bay in the quiet understanding care of Edward.

The room returned to its unique stillness, which is a void that consists of a nightly chorus of human dreams, bodily functions and even the odd unidentifiable rumbling. My world began to return to normal and my heart slowed its frantic race against my heaving ribcage. Although tired, I realised that sleep would not come quickly after such an event so I headed off to the toilet and a leg stretch along the corridor. Edward successfully returned the women to her bed and settled her down. He came from her bay and saw me in the corridor, realising I was now properly awake he offered me a cup of tea which I gratefully accepted before heading back to my own bed. As I waited I switched on my bedside lamp and decided to read for a while. Edward brought my drink and enquired if I was OK and did I want anything else? I replied I was fine and thanked him for his concern for both myself and the old lady. I then settled down to my book, sat at the top of my bed so I could see to read in the dim light cast by the bedside lamp.

Eventually after supping the tea and calming myself with the aid of a short read, I decided it was time to attempt sleep. As quietly as possible I laid down my book, careful to mark the page, and reached to switch off the lamp. That done I pushed my feet down under the covers as I began to relax myself down for what remained of the very short hospital night. Down into the cool bedclothes slipped my feet, closely followed obviously by my legs, but then, horror! I snatched my body out of the bed in an instant, my face mirroring the disgust at what I had found. The old woman had left me a gift. While sitting at the bottom of my bed, the poor sad old lady had quietly wet herself and my bed!

For the second time that night I reached for the nurse call button . . . . .!

Chapter Two: Tales from a lift (*Elevator*) . . . .

Following a life time of hospital treatment, both as an inpatient and an outpatient, I have made countless trips to hospitals up and down the country. Some hospitals are very modern and efficient, others show the worn signs of years serving the sick and injured in the community. Some hospital designers considering the very modern hospital and its resources still strive to put the patient last in the list of priorities. Long corridors, hidden lifts and mountains of stairs, all strategically placed to confuse and bewilder the poor patient or visitor. From car parks to wards, from restaurants to clinics, finding ones way in the mystifying halls of medical supremacy can be daunting. However, it is often the very people wandering these halls that prove to be the most amusing, or confusing.

One of my most recent adventures involved a weekly trip to a hospital situated in a neighbouring county, about 45 minutes drive away. The treatment I was to receive was not pleasant and I certainly did not look forward to either the long drive or the necessary pain and discomfort of the administered medication. However it had been decreed that this particular treatment was important to my continue health, and in fact my every existence so I continued to make the trip to and from the hospital every week. Although the trip was quite long for me, it was mostly straight forward and somewhat boring. I hate driving and only do it because I hate public transport even more, and worse than that, I hate having to use my legs! Someone once said in a moment of pure philosophy;

"Do not run if you can walk, do not walk if you can stand, do not stand if you can sit, and do not sit if you can lie down."

I believe in this philosophy!

On this particular day my trip up to the hospital had usually been very uneventful. I had not gotten lost which was always a good sign, nor had I crashed or even slightly dented my car or anyone else's. A successful road journey made without mishap, but still just enough to initiate my slide into a foul mood. Arriving at the hospital I then faced the arduous chore of seeking and securing the ever elusive parking space. After some time spent circling the car park like a vulture over a carcass, I noticed one old gent just getting into his vehicle.

'Are you about to go?' I enquired.

Upon receiving a positive reply I positioned my car in order to accept the space immediately after he vacated it. I needed to make certain no other vehicle would jump in ahead of me, as happens quite frequently in cities I have noticed. Sure enough, just as I began to reverse into the space, another vehicle attempted to pinch it from me by driving in nose first! I am delighted to say I won this minor battle. Motorcars have always been just a simple form of transport to me; I really do not care what they look like just as long as they get me safely from A to B without too many breakdowns or disasters. Therefore I have no concerns about the odd dent or scratch on my vehicle. Happily the other driver obviously wanted to keep his shiny motor in pristine condition as I noticed a look of fright flee across his features. Also in my favour was the fact that mine is quite a big car and must have appeared threatening as it rolled unstoppably towards my intended destination. I accelerated slightly and did not falter as I continued my manoeuvre into the space, causing the other driver to rapidly reverse and back off, gesturing as he drove off in search of another parking space, much to my satisfaction. Once parked, locked up and content that I was well within the lines of the parking bay, I decided a coffee could be the order of the day. Off I set towards the restaurant, anticipating a few minutes rest and refreshment before I headed off to the chamber of torture.

I did not have to walk too far to the hospital main entrance. However it still took longer than it should as I was forced to avoid mothers with prams and babies, walking frames wielded threateningly by old people with attitude and smokers trying to flatten themselves against a discreet wall, while dragging heavily on their cigarettes and hoping no one would notice them. Doctors and nurses flew past me, steadfastly avoiding any form of eye contact in case you were a patient and frightened you would bother them in their time off or lunch period. Young people thumbing their mobile phones frantically as if the whole world was going to end any moment and it was vitally important they sent a text to as many friends as possible before this major event occurred. Finally there were those who stare off into space and do not notice you or anyone else's presence as they walk doggedly towards their vehicle or to await public transport. Everyone avoids these people, the poker faced, tight lipped individuals that move forward as if in a trance. There are two kinds of poker face, those walking into the hospital with their mind full of worries. And those exiting from the hospital with the answers they did not want to hear. Everyone avoids these unfortunate people.

Frustrated I eventually reached the hospital entrance and headed for the restaurant and found myself at the very end of a long, long queue. It appeared the whole population of the country, along with their friends and relatives were in place in front of me. All I wanted was a coffee and a bun of some description. But so did all those standing patiently in the long line of people that snaked around the hospital lobby before even entering the restaurant! I gave up at this point and decided to search out the department I needed within the hospital, so off I set, my mood now despondent.

Of course it did not help when I tried to make my way to Level Three where the department I sought was located. Never having been to this area of the hospital before, I dutifully read all the directions signs and headed off like an intrepid explorer. As I was already on Level Six, I followed the signs until I found the stairs down, I rarely use lifts going down, only those going up due to my persistent dislike of physical effort. Down the flights of stairs I went, logic telling me Level Three would be situated beneath Level Six, and happy to be heading towards my destination with no undue cause for concern, I eventually arrived at Level Four. Lo and behold, no sign of Level Three! I had reached a dead end. The stairs now only went back up! No sign or direction for Level Three anywhere in view, just a strange ward entrance, stairs that went up and two blank walls.

Panic was now beginning to creep its way towards me, 'where the hell do I go from here?' I wondered. Thankfully a vision appeared in front of me, a young nurse who appeared to know where she was even if I did not.

'Excuse me,' I said as calmly as possible, not wanting to impress I was totally lost, 'Can you tell me how I get to Level Three from here please?'

Ha ha, big joke! The nurse looked at me and smiled, yep I was only one amongst a multitude that had fallen into this dastardly trap laid by those all intelligent architects and builders. Still smiling but with a faint attitude of resignation, the young nurse dutifully gave me directions before she headed off into the myriad of corridors and obscurity. Level Three does not follow Level Four; in fact Level Three is in an entire different part of the hospital and can only be reached from that particular section of the hospital. Level Four is a dead end and Level Three is somewhere else entirely. Hurray for modern hospital design!

With just a few tears, off I went in my continued search for the elusive Level Three, back up the stairs because I did not know where the lifts where or if there ever were any lifts at all on Level Four. Climbed, staggered and crawled back up to Level Six and started again. After many moments of questioning innocent passersby, hospital staff, policemen and all other assorted unknowledgeable strangers, I eventually found access to Level Three via an almost hidden sign. It pointed towards a small corridor and stated that lifts to Level Three were located here, so I decided I would use the lifts this time, if only out of concern for my rapidly declining health after already surmounting several flights of stairs.

In the discreet corner of a nameless corridor lurked the elusive lift bay, which I gratefully entered. I was stood alone waiting for the lift to arrive, I had obviously pressed the desired button and the lift was creaking its way down to me. There were six lifts and I assumed that pressing one button would automatically call the nearest one to my destination. I choose the lift door that seemed an appropriate place to wait and stood patiently when suddenly an old woman pushed right in front of me and viciously stabbed the button again! No words spoken, no 'Excuse me'; nothing! She had marched up to the lift control panel and jabbed a bony finger at the already pressed and illuminated lift call button before standing back to wait. As if I would be standing there waiting for a lift to arrive by chance! Maybe she considered me a dimwit who was simply standing in front of a lift door with an unused call button within my reach but had not the intelligence to use it.

A few minutes later another person joined us and again stabbed the very same button. About four more people turned up and every one of them pressed the same button! Why? The damn thing was light up to indicate it had been pressed already, so why did everyone feel the over whelming need to push it again? I was thinking to myself that if I was a professional comedian, I could do an excellent running joke on this weird behaviour. Things got even sillier.

Eventually the lift finally arrived, the doors opened with a swish and a groan and we all climbed aboard. Guess what? Yep, every single person who entered the lift at that floor and at that time pressed the same button inside the lift for the exact same floor! I think at the final count there were about seven of us all going to the same floor, and as each person entered the lift, they all reached out, often having to nudge someone aside, and jabbed at the button again.

I could not fail to see the humour in this mechanical behaviour, a conviction that strengthened as I clearly saw everyone, all those packed into the stuffy, airless lift were heading for the same floor as me, and the damn button was light up like a beacon. I did not bother to even go near the button. The other passengers trapped in the metal box of the lift stared at me with incomprehension etched into their faces. Why hadn't he pressed the button? Where was he going? All these thoughts were clearing whizzing round the heads of those fellow passengers as they pondered the abnormality of my actions, or rather my lack of actions. Spontaneously the moments pondering had concluded, then as one entity every one of them shuffled round to face the steel doors and became still, none spoke a word. Even those who were talking before entering the lift became quiet. The passengers appeared to hold a silent vigil while awaiting release by the swish of the twin mechanical sliding doors.

At this point I did consider copying the famous Peter Sellers moment from one of his films. That scene showed a lift packed full of comedy gangster types, each one trying to keep a straight face when someone broke wind loudly in the crowded lift, but I came to the conclusion that the other passengers may not understand, appreciate, hear or smell the joke!

We reached Level Three and the vigil at the doors was over, everyone aboard the lift exited as swiftly as feasible. Possibly all were secretly afraid the lift would spirit them all off to destinations unknown, or worse still, another mysterious location within the rambling hospital maze. With the final exodus the world returned to normal and almost all the passengers immediately began talking again. Weird!

Eventually after leaving the lift to disappear off in its quest to transport more unsuspecting travellers to destinations unknown, I ultimately reached my intended department and once more did my impression of a human colander and or dart board, although not until the condition of my breathing had caused some consternation. Laughing, climbing stairs and watching these sheep like people had by now almost done me in!

Two hours of needle pricking, injections and other assorted medical pleasures, the treatment was over and I was free, retracing my steps I headed for the lift again. I felt sure that the inhibited behaviour from the morning could not possibly repeat itself, surly the vast intelligence of the human race could not be generically identified as lift fearing sheep? Alas yes, the exact same sequence happened all over again. Everyone pressed the same button to call the lift, everyone pressed the same button for the same floor, everyone turned to face the door and no one spoke.

This time I decided I had to do something, the situation simply cried out for a humorous interlude. I slowly and unobtrusively edged my way towards the rear of the lift, a move made easy by the combined effort of my fellow passengers as they surged gently nearer those hallowed steel doors. Once in position I gave some thought on the best possible action I could take in order to achieve the best possible results. Deciding that breaking wind as in the Peter Sellers film may be slightly OTT, I concluded the next best thing would be to take advantage of the panic recently spread by the threat of Bird Flu, Swine Flu or other assorted animal coughs and colds. All those adverts and posters of the time warning people to *Catch it, Bin it and Destroy it!*

In the silence of the moving lift, I began to cough, not just a gentle cough but a hacking, rasping cough intermixed with as many groans and sniffles as I could manage. I coughed and I hawked as if trying to shift some particularly stubborn phlegm from the deepest, darkest, nastiest corners of my lungs. My face became a bright red, my shoulders heaved and my hankie waved everywhere except in front of my mouth. I think I possibly over did it a little bit; I must have looked like I had a form of rabid flu rather than possible swine flu!

But it worked! Everyone in the lift immediately took a hurried step away from me. Even those with little space to move appeared to suddenly find an extra inch of room. I was stood leaning against the rail at the back of the lift, trying not to laugh out loud between coughs, chokes and gasps, as all those poor silent worshippers of the steel doors moved desperately forward, moving away from me as one body. I am positive those at the very front had their noses pressed tight up against the doors as those behind pushed foreword in an effort to distance themselves from me. When the doors finally opened at the chosen floor, the rush to get out equalled that of a Boxing Day sale. In an instant I was standing alone in the lift as if no one else had ever been there! My entire group of fellow passengers had fled in every direction, fleeing the untold horror that that assailed them on their quiet lift journey.

At this point the thought struck that what if I had really been ill? What if my prank was genuine? No one offered the slightest concern or help at my apparent predicament, their only concern was to escape the vicinity of the coughing wreak in the corner of the lift. Would the realization hit them later? Would they wonder if I was alive or dead? If help had arrived or was I still lying prone at the rear of the lift as it continued its soulless journeys between the numerous and mysterious floors of the hospital? Personally I doubt it, from the looks of distain on their faces I believe my fellow travellers had washed me from their minds as quickly as they washed their hands!

These events may have lowered my opinion of the modern day hospital lift passengers, and their collective inability to think as an individual, and showing the uncaring and selfish side to our human nature. Or possibly it was a basic herding instinct and the need to flock together for safety in the face of a hideous threat. But it certainly brightened my day. Who knew visiting a hospital could provide so much entertainment?

Or be so thought provoking?

Chapter Three: Wetting the bed.

The old chap who lay quietly in his bed confused everyone. He could speak clearly, hear reasonably well, was aware of his surroundings and his environment. He was obviously unfazed by his time in hospital and his family visited often and kept him well stocked with snacks, fruit and soft drinks. In general he was an amicable ward mate, pleasant and polite to both fellow patients and nursing staff. He appeared to be heading into his eighties but at this time was noticeably not well and did sometimes seem slightly confused. A slim man who showed the tell tale signs of having lived a full life but who's allotted time was now beginning to wind down.

As a patient he was quite normal, only reaching for the nurse call button if he could not achieve a chore or action himself, or if none of us could answer his plea for assistance. Not that he asked for much, he seemed content to lie in his hospital bed and watch as his confined world revolved around him. He was not able to walk or get out of bed solely due to his present health, but for the most he managed quite well, not imposing on the busy nurses or fellow patients. In fact he was what could be called an ideal patient, except for one thing, he constantly wet his bed!

No one understood why he kept wetting his bed, he frequently requested a urine bottle or bedpan, which ever was relevant and was obviously aware of when the need to relieve himself arose. So why did he wet his bed so often? A question the nurses wished they had the answer for as they were constantly involved in changing his soaking bedclothes, sheets and blankets. Being that the patient was bed bound and unable to even sit up properly, this task was always arduous, the nurses having to manually shift him around the bed while they stripped and changed the bed linen and his pyjamas and washed him countless times both day and night.

The other patients in the ward joked that he was a bit too old to be still wetting his bed; did his mother not teach him how to use a toilet? Maybe he didn't like touching the thing? Perhaps we should tie a bell to it so he could ring for help? All the raucous jibes and jokes that were meant in good heart but were also intended to prompt him into either stopping the bed wetting or seeking help whenever he felt the need to go. The poor chap was noticeably embarrassed by his actions but took all the jokes in good heart. He continually insisted he had no idea why his efforts to use the simple urine bottle eluded him. He often joked himself that maybe he could not reach, maybe the bottle was too big for him, and perhaps it would be better if he had a catheter fitted? Whatever the problem was, it was not for the want of trying to manage and his efforts and confusion only added to the comical scene he portrayed. We all felt generally sorry for the poor guy.

One day it came to our notice that he always reported his wet bed immediately after requesting a urine bottle. So then the discussions centred on; 'shaking off those last drops before pulling out' or 'Use a bottle that does not leak next time'. Being a gentleman of the old school he refused to have a nurse help him while he toileted, not an action some of us younger patients would have turned down, life can be very boring in hospitals. Not wishing to embarrass him but eager to identify the problem, we all secretly agreed to watch his actions when he next used the bottle, but alas to no avail. He always followed the same routine. After requesting and receiving a bottle he would discreetly lift his bed covers, insert the bottle in place and cover his self up again while he performed his duty. Nothing seemed amiss but yet again, once he had carefully removed the bottle from between his legs, he called for the nurses to change his now wet bed.

Finally we could bear it no longer; we had to discover the cause of this poor bloke's toiletry misfortunes. So in the quiet period between lunch and visiting time we convinced him to mime his entire routine when attempting to pee into a bottle. With great embarrassment he agreed and began to demonstrate exactly what he did. First he lowered the covers so we could all see. He then reluctantly mimed fumbling for his manhood as he laid the bottle in its position ready for use with his other hand. The fumbling continued as he carefully lined himself up and placed the bottle in its appropriate place. We all stared in amazement as he emphasised each move so we could all clearly see his actions. I must point out for the sake of decency that through all this the guy remained fully clothed and not once did he actually remove his genitals from his pyjamas bottoms!

The old guy was now enjoying himself, entering into the spirit of theatre along with all those in the ward. I am sure that sometime in his past he had been involved in amateur dramatics or some form of stage performance. He dutifully mimed each action, even managing to form a look of relief on his face as he acted out the actions of urination. After some melodramatic gestures and over stated sighs and groans, he proceeded to remove the bottle from its location between his legs and very carefully placed it on his bedside table.

He looked round at each one of us, his expression asking the question he dearly wanted to know, we in turn stared back at him in bewilderment.

His curiosity at its peak, he at last shouted, 'Well? Why don't you say something? What's the matter? Come on; tell me, what's wrong?'

None of us could speak! We had all seen and identified the mistake he was continually making in blissful unawareness. At once the hilarity burst forth. Tears rolled down our faces and nurses came running into the ward in response to the sudden rush of noise emanating from the room. Coughing and gasping quickly follow the raucous laughter, causing the bemused nurses to utter soothing noises in an attempt to calm us down, looks of concern flowing across their faces. Eventually we regained our breath and our senses as we sucked on our oxygen masks and dabbed at our eyes with paper tissues. The truth was out, we all knew the answer to the poor chaps embarrassing problem.

The standard male urine bottle is designed with a spout tilting up at an approximate angle of 45 degrees. This allows the man to insert himself into the bottle easily while the bottle rests securely on the bed and allows the fluid to run freely down into the main body of the bottle. The lifted angle of the bottle neck also aids the safe movement of the bottle while keeping any accidental spillage to a minimum. The bottom of the bottle is flat so it can be laid on a mattress without rolling or moving about, the main body is rounded in girth and oval in length before tapering into the raised tubular construction of the bottle neck. The shape of hospital urine bottles has not changed much since their invention, only the material from which they are constructed has differed over the years. From the original metal that often caused sudden shocks to the user, frequently resulting in a premature dribble or full on flow before the poor user could regain control. Shocks in the most inappropriate place caused by the metal bottles either being too cold, cold metal between ones legs. Or scalding hot from being only recently removed form a sterilising unit, hot metal between ones legs.

Not sure which I would prefer! Let your imagination ponder on the two choices for a moment, which would you prefer?

Then on to the ever favourite plastic bottle, common in the age when plastic appeared to rule the world, and finally to the modern day compressed recycled cardboard. These cardboard urine bottles and bedpans are not as daft as they may sound, the reasons of use obviously included hygiene, and the used toiletry implements can be disposed of complete with contents, thus removing the need for sterilising and the risks involved in multiple uses. But I suspect the main reason the cardboard bottles and bedpans now replace both metal and plastic, is purely down to cost. They are cheap to produce and disposable. Easy!

I have included this description as I am aware that these pieces of equipment are not to be found in the normal every day home, office or school. It is equipment found in every hospital, nursing home or hospice, any venue where people may not have the ability to commute to a toilet, be it through ill health, old age or disability. It is a fact that many people do not even know such things exist, hence this description for those lucky enough not to have ever needed to use such a device.

The hilarity in the ward quickly ceased while the nurses looked on in confusion, followed by demands for an explanation from both the staff and the poor gent upon whom all the attention centred. The other patients all turned to look at me, making it perfectly clear that I had been elected to give the poor chap the explanation. With a deep breath and as poker faced as possible, I requested a new bottle from the staff so I could better give an account of his misguided actions for all to see. I then slowly and carefully explained to the old guy how the bottle should be used, much to the nurse's impatience as like us, considered the method of using a urine bottle was obvious. Being somewhat of an extrovert, I happily mimed the toiletry actions of the old guy so the nurses could also appreciate the humour, though the poor patient was still lingering in the dark and very bemused as the humour in the situation became apparent.

At this point I must point out that the elderly gentleman was not in anyway short in his mental ability, he was intelligent and quick witted, but perhaps not as familiar with; 'these new fangled gadgets' as the rest of us. Also I believe this was his first admission to hospital following an active and healthy life, so he lacked the experience of we frequent inmates of the health service.

Finally, when his patience and good humour began to run out, I began explaining to him where he was going wrong. Holding up the new (unused) urine bottle, I demonstrated the correct way to use this piece of vital medical equipment while exaggerating my proportions for the amusement of the nurses and ridicule of the patients. Immediately realisation, followed rapidly by a red glow of embarrassment lit up his features. As I mimed the action of using a bottle it became very obvious that he had been using the bottle upside down! Everything he put in simply ran straight back out, either while in the process of urinating or during the following action of lifting the bottle out from beneath his bed covers.

'I wondered why the damn thing was so difficult to use, I could not understand why the neck faced down when my little friend wanted to face up. I just thought it was designed in a stupid way. Sorry!' explained the patient to the nurses and fellow patients, 'You must think I'm a right plonker!'

'At least you managed to use the bedpan right, or that would have been interesting!' a nurse quipped as they returned to their duties, laughing.

29

The problem was solved, to the delight of the poor over worked nurses who had long ago grown tired of continually changing the guy's bed, and to the continued embarrassment of the poor old fellow himself.

Chapter four: Noisy nights

Sleeping through the night when in hospital is often a truly difficult task, sleeping soundly and undisturbed at night in a full hospital ward is nigh on impossible! Not only must one contend with the strange and unfamiliar surroundings and an unfamiliar and uncomfortable bed, one must also endure the strange sights, sounds, and smells that percolate silently or are blown around the room in gusts during the dead of night. All this of course is in addition to any health issues, pain or discomfort that is already making sleep difficult.

Let your imagination run riot as you picture a room full of sleeping gentlemen of varying ages and physical constitutions. Snores ripple against the ears like a tidal wave of pneumatic road drills. Grunts and coughs pierce the darkness like the cries of some alien monster lurking in the shadows. The rustling of bedclothes and whispered curses as a backside becomes exposed to the cool air, or feet chill with the loss of cover at the bottom of the bed. Snippets of dream held conversations with past friends or replaying past events can be detected from the sleep talkers. The crackling of crisp packets, chocolate wrappers or biscuits accompany the clicking of false teeth and lay witness to a night time feast by those that simply cannot wait until breakfast, or others who just cannot sleep. On occasion there can the heard the mournful cry of those in pain or suffering, increasing to a crescendo, sporadically succeeded by the patter of nurses flat shoes rushing to quell the noise and attempt to humanely ease the agonies of the sufferer. Or of course silence the noisy blighter before he or she wakens the whole ward and totally destroys any chance of a quiet night shift at work!

Noises originate from other sources, excluding the patients themselves. The movement and chatter of the night nurses as they go about their chores and duties, the ping of the staff kitchen microwave as it heats the packaged meals or soups that nourish the staff during the long night shift. The rattle of cups and the tinkling of tea spoons stirring those endless mugs of tea, coffee, hot chocolate or cocktails necessary to remain conscious, even if only semiconscious during the dark hours. These days with the addition of computers to hospitals and especially the wards, the sound of clicking keys accompanied by the excited discussions on where one should go for a holiday, what was being sold via online auction or who had commented on one of the social networking sites.

Doctors it seems cannot remain quiet when on night duty. Once summoned they barge onto the ward hours later through the obligatory creaking twin swing doors, keys clinking from their belts and mobile phones and personal pagers bleeping at the highest volume setting. Unlike the nurses, doctors can sport whatever foot wear they choose; the more fashion conscious click along the corridors in Cuban heels or squeaking training shoes on the males, female doctors appear to favour high heels or those very annoying 'flip-flop' sandals, what ever choice of shoe is decided upon, all hit the hard, linoleum floors as the junior medics rush importantly onto the ward.

The sound of foot wear is promptly followed by a screech as a chair is dragged unceremoniously across the floor as the doctor places him or her self in front of a computer in an attempt to gain wisdom into a patient's condition. Once satisfied they have absolutely no idea about the patient's state of health, they then proceed to the unfortunate patient's bedside and attempt an often one sided conversation in the loudest whisper known to man. This conversation invariably requires illumination, rustling of patient notes and calls for assistance from a nurse. Often the doctor is accompanied by a trolley or tray containing syringes, stethoscopes, and vials of medication and assorted other frightening instruments that gleam evilly in the glare of the bedside lamp. It is never enough! These is always some item of medication, some vital instrument or piece of paperwork forgotten that requires the doctor to rush frantically from the ward in search of the missing item, usually several times.

Once the harassed teenage looking doctor is satisfied he/she has all the treatment requirements, the tray holding the apparatus is invariably dropped. Or the trolley itself over turned. So the procedure begins once again. Off rushes the doctor for replacement medication, more instruments and thumbscrews. Already over worked nurses rally to his/her aid in an effort to get the patient attended to and the doctor off the ward as soon as possible, thus allowing the now disturbed patients to get some sleep.

The treatment finally begins on a patient who has no comprehension as to why a strange person is talking to them, asking questions and prodding their bodies in a most intrusive manner. A confused and bewildered attempt is made by the patient to answer the issued questions that are as unfamiliar or as incomprehensible as a rocket science manual or a politician's expenses claim form. Finally the unwitting patient is shot into full consciousness as the first of many needles is stabbed into one of his limbs. At last the assault is concluded and without a word the doctor vanishes from the ward, safe in the certain knowledge that he/she has successfully treated yet another poor soul. The patient lies in confusion, fear and astonishment, left wondering what the heck just happened!

One of the most common causes of noise disturbance during the night hours on a hospital ward is the constant ringing of phones. I have often wondered who makes so many phone calls to a hospital ward in the dead of night, and more importantly; why? With the majority of hospital staff off duty and likely enjoying a more peaceful night than the patients, visitors and general hangers on excluded from the property, doctors habitually elusive, and administration personnel not even aware that the hospital continues to operate outside the hours of nine till five. Management staff go about their respective night time routines blissfully unaware that the world does indeed continue to revolve without them!

Similar to those frustrating and annoying occurrences that happen at home when ever one endeavours to bathe or shower or even consider those important bodily functions that always require immediate attention. As soon as ones feet are wet or one is comfortably installed in the smallest room armed with newspapers or magazines, the phone will ring. As in hospital at night, the phone will inevitably begin ringing when the nurses are located at the farthest part of the ward and busy with a patient. The caller then sits on the end of the line, the phone rings on and on for an eternity, disturbing all with its piecing voice. I have often been tempted to get up and answer these night time calls, I am sure I could think of something to say to the irritating person on the other end of the line. Possibly impolite but certainly to the point!

Illumination can be a huge hindrance to the would be unconscious patient, bed side lights left on by late readers, or switched on for easy observation of an especially poorly patient or simply not switched off by the unaware user who had fallen asleep. Light floods in from the corridors and the nurses station, light from other parts of the building shines majestically from one room into another within visual range, and external light seeps in through insufficiently drawn curtains or blinds, allowing the glare from street lights and car headlights to stab through the darkness, and usually right into ones eyes!

All these are light sources that we have little control over I admit, but the one that does require a comment is the night nurse with a torch. With illumination from internal and external environments, actually seeing where one is walking is relatively easy in a hospital ward, but when it comes to examining a prone patient to ensure natural sleep rather than sickness induce coma requires a greater level of candle power. Most night nursing staff carry a torch of some description to allow them clear visibility of patients and this fact is completely understandable and even commendable. Unfortunately one does encounter the odd nurse with a fetish for ripping patients awake with a blinding light piercing their eye lids. This act of shining a bright light directly in another's vision appears to be a human trait, give anyone a torch and the first thing they do in return is turn its full beam into your eyes! I have never understood this action but it is a fact of life, give a person a source of illumination and they will immediately direct its beam into your face and particularly, your eyes. So even if one manages to sleep through the noise and unwanted illumination, a further obstacle to prolonged sleep is the very person who's employed to protect your health and well being while in their care, the nurse and her torch.

Those of you who have been misfortunate enough to have required an admission and stay in hospital will also be aware of one other factor known to disturb and otherwise restful night. I cannot speak for a ward full of women, but I certainly can for a ward full of men. Men of all ages, medical conditions, appetites and constitutions enclosed together in a room at night can constitute a hazard normally unmentioned in polite society. And what is this hazard? The smell!

Rich aromas floating on the night air and creating a heady perfume of old socks, unwashed feet; sweaty bodies, urine bottles, stale aftershave, decomposition and the gaseous eruptions from previous meals and snacks, the burps and farts. There is nowhere one can escape this assail, unrestrained, unreserved and unidentifiable fragrances from the deepest, darkness pit of humanity invade the darkness. In silent and deadly assaults or with thunderous approval, these gagging odours can jerk a person awake faster than a bottle of smelling salts!

Many factors combine to keep sleep at bay in a modern hospital ward, some factors relate simply to the environment while others originate from being human. In all said and done, these are natural and excepted disturbances that are not solely indigenous to hospital wards, most of these conditions can be found in other venues where people gather in one room to sleep. Army barracks, boarding schools, prisons; government offices, Parliament, university lecture halls and especially retirement or homeless hostels. But there is one factor not mentioned before that rears its noisy head particularly in hospital wards, mainly because retribution is frowned upon in an otherwise caring institution. This factor is human and concerns the ability to talk!

Everyone has had at least one experience on a bus, or train or may be even on a plane, though I believe this is not their normally identified habitat. The one person to be avoided at all costs on public transport, the eccentric guy or lady.

The irrational individual who strives to sit beside you on a bus or seeks you out in a train and engage you in an illogical conversation while managing to converse with themselves at the same time. The person whom every other passenger prays will choose someone else, not them. The individual, whose habits and conversational topics leave you stunned, shunned and absolutely perplexed with the incoherent babble, remnants of a powerful body odour and complete absence of rational thought.

It is these special people that appear in the silent wards at night. Patients' who manage to sleep peacefully throughout the daylight hours suddenly burst awake immediately the main lights are extinguished. Ailments, pains and all manner of agonies rise to the fore as these nocturnal patients give vent to their nightly cries. In their sick and fevered minds the cries ring out for mothers, fathers, sisters, brothers, wives, girlfriends, boyfriends, both, and occasionally the call for a nurse. Beseeching all from the past or present to come and bring an end to their private tortures. Agonies made vocal and amplified by irrational, confused and disturbed minds join the multitude of acoustics that punish the silence of the night.

Understanding and empathy and even pity must be considered here, for those who are suffering in either mind or body while their biological systems attempt the necessary repairs. But it is not the suffering of the sick I refer to now, it is that peculiar person, the one from the bus, the same one from the train, the one who has followed you into the sanctuary of the hospital ward. There appears to be one of these in every ward I have every frequented. The particular patient who constantly demands attention, from requiring replacement urine bottles to the straightening of sheets. From bed pans to cups of tea, to seeking lights on or off, to reaching spectacles accessible within easy grasp, enquiring the correct spelling of a word chosen in a puzzle, opening a packet of biscuits or moving an item placed on the bed side table from one area of clutter to the next. Requests for help or assistance that are totally unnecessary, utterly unimportant and a complete waste of time.

By far the most common of these thoroughly useless demands on a busy nurses work load concerns what time of night it is, repeatedly every five minutes brings the same request until the poor nurse simply refuses to answer. Even the smallest request is shouted at full volume by these individuals, insignificant tasks searched for and identified as a means of attention. The desire to announce their presence to fellow patients and staff alike, and to anyone within a five mile radius!

One particular gent was ensconced on my ward during my last visit. I forget his name, mainly because we came up with several of our own for him. At first appearance he seemed to be a mild mannered and polite aged hippy. But we soon discovered different.

In some major modern hospitals, the designers and architects naively concluded that small windows, an insufficient air flow and over active central heating system was the requirement of all those sick or injured. So many hospital wards become unacceptably hot, stuffy and claustrophobic during the summer months. Patients swelter on plastic covered mattresses, medical staff perspiring by the gallon as they rush about in the course of their duties, and visitors stagger as they are hit by a wall of heat when they arrive on the ward from the cool corridors and fresh outdoor air.

But apparently immune to the heat and discomfort, this particular gent insisted on numerous blankets as he lay in a mummified position wrapped tightly against any possible threat of draft or drop in temperature that may invade his cocoon. All that could be seen was his head, long untidy hair and beard appearing like cheap tobacco spilling from the end of a human joint or spliff, a narcotic cigarette! There he would lay, snug in his envelop of blankets while those around him sweltered in the stuffy heat. But he did not sleep. His calls for the nurse were constant throughout the night, his demands for attention bordered on torture for both patients and night staff. His pleas for help or assistance were a sham, not once did he actually require any medical help or comfort. His demands ranged from moving an item on his bed table, because he considered it to be out of place, to brushing his own long hair away from his eyes, to counting his few coins, left on his bedside table in readiness for the morning newspaper round.

When the night staff decided to ignore him, and we patients threatened to gag him, he found another method of making himself heard. He began talking back to his hospital radio. At first they were just mutterings but it was not long before he was ranting and raving at what ever programme he was listening to over his headphones. Nurses rushed in to our ward, thinking some poor soul in dire need of help, or an unfortunate patient in the grip of a horrific nightmare. No, it was the old hippy, making sure all in the immediate vicinity were aware of his presence!

The poor nurses have to be polite and caring towards their patients. They tried in vain to convince the hippy to remain quiet for the benefit of the other patients. He replied in amazement that no noise was coming from him. He was only venting his opinion to a chat programme on the radio and considered his volume of voice to be acceptable for the situation. The concept of considering the sleep requirements of those sharing his ward obviously never entered his mind. The nurses were forced to leave, dejected in their failure. But not the patients . . . .

As soon as the nurses had left the ward, we acted. With an unspoken agreement three of we more capable patients left our beds and approached the hippy. Without a word I reached up and switched off his bedside radio before removing his headphones and placing them out of reach. A second patient pried the nurse call handset from the hippies sweating grasp and placed that too out of reach. But it was the third patient who had the most profound effect on the noisy hippy. Without a single word the burly patient looked directly into the hippies face, indicated a rolled sock in his huge hand and with gestures made it very plain where he would insert the sock if any further sound omitted from the hippies mouth. In truth I think it was this action alone that ensured the rest of our night was peaceful!

Finally in a world seemingly full of nightly distractions come the monitors. These are machines placed beside a patient's bed and monitor important health responses such as heart rate, respiratory rate, pulse, oxygen saturation and blood pressure. These machines are an obvious necessity in maintaining close observation on a particularly sick patient, and no one would begrudge their use. Regrettably these machines omit a loud bleep! They bleep constantly when in use, day or night. But even this is acceptable because it allows the staff and doctors to hear that all is well with the patient, or not well if the bleep stops or changes its pitch, speed or tone, notifying the medical staff that the patient requires attention, thus dismissing the need for a continued visual vigilance.

Another form of monitor can be found skulking in hospital wards, is a machine which regulates the speed of delivery of an intravenous infusion, commonly known as a *drip*. Monitors attached to this apparatus warn nurses if the infusion is interrupted, the line removed by a confused patient, or that the medication bottle is near to empty. Again these machines serve a purpose and must be accepted as an integral part of modern medicine. The sleep busting issues arise with the machines sensitivity. Often all the patient needs to do is shift his or her arm into a more comfortable sleeping position and the monitor will begin screeching its alarm! Bending ones arm, laying on an arm, even attempting to place the limb under the bed covers can result in that mind numbing, teeth clenching continuous and monotonous bleep that penetrates ones consciousness like a form of water torture or a politicians long winded ramble in reply to a question he has no intention of answering.

Regular patients with the understanding of such modern medical machines know to quickly move their offending limb back to its numbingly uncomfortable position and the bleeping alarm will cease. Those patients unaware of this procedure or simply too ill to understand, too sick to move or those lucky people who can sleep through an earthquake or especially those patients too inconsiderate to care send these machines into a screaming frenzy throughout the night. Nurses try to quell the disruption but to little avail, sleeping people do and always will fling their limbs in a variety of directions and positions in bed.

So while these machines add to the audio disruption in the dark hours between meals, no one really complains. Except the peculiar guy! There is always at least one patient known for shouting requests to *'turn the bloody telly off'* as it is keeping him awake!

The moral of these stories conclude that if one is unfortunate enough to be admitted into a large hospital in the twenty first century, please be aware that sleep is best achieved during daylight hours. The nights are noisy, bright; disturbed, interrupted or too entertaining for sleep to be considered.

Chapter Five: The man who would not eat . . .

Sometimes the personal habits or marginality of an individual patient will provide amusement or interest to an otherwise monotonous hospital ward. Each of us have our own oddities, our own beliefs and our own fears, any one of these may appear bizarre to another person, but they are ours and we love, nurture and retain them no matter what others might say or think. It is said that each of us have a minor form of autism within us, responsible for little quirks in our life style. For example, those who insist on maintaining a strict routine at home, hanging washing out on the line to dry in perfect order, towels in one group, sheets in another, jeans together and *smalls* at the end. Those who clean their cars beginning driver's side first, those who do not like touching other people, and of course those that like to touch other people, sometimes way too much! A famous tennis player was observed by the world as he carefully and precisely positioned each of his two drinks bottles in exactly the same way for each match. There are many names for such odd behaviour, quirkiness, weird streak, peculiarities or even mentally insane but what ever this unordinary behaviour is; we all have our own personal fad. If you are rich then it's called eccentricity!

There is often an underlying cause for such strange behaviour or beliefs, and this root cause can be stranger still, sometimes defying explanation. In the majority of cases, this idiosyncrasy is as individual as a finger print and can be so insignificant that the person and those around them remain in ignorance. On occasion a peculiarity rears its head and stares the world in the face, challenging all to defy it.

The chap in the bed next to me caused some concern on the ward with his strange dietary foible. He was quite an elderly guy who appeared in the main to still be reasonably fit and able. Gray hair topped a round face, a solid figure now softened by age and medium height. A pleasant fellow, polite and friendly but was obviously suffering the obligatory lack of audio response that accompanies most of us into our twilight years. I did not know why he was in hospital but I soon gathered he was on the road to recovery and expected to be discharged very soon.

Aside from his health issues that originally landed him in hospital, his only real problem appeared when ever food or drink was presented to him. From information gained from the other patients, he was already a patient before I was admitted into the hospital; he had hardly eaten or drunk anything since he had been admitted. At first everyone naturally assumed his appetite would improve once his health improved, no one feels like eating much when feeling ill and totally out of sorts.

My first real impression of this trait grew evident when the drinks trolley came trundling out with the afternoon teas, coffees and hot chocolates. The cheerful tea lady asked him if he wanted a cup of tea.

'Er, no,' he said quietly.

'Coffee then?'

'No,' he said again.

'Hot chocolate?'

'No.'

'Well; what would you like to drink?' asked the tea lady, getting slightly annoyed.

I admit I was surprised at his constant refusal. Food and drink of any description become the highlight of the day when stuck in a mindlessly boring hospital ward. Like trained circus animals, each and every one of us would prepare ourselves and sit by our bed tables in drooling anticipation of each meal or hot drink. Not that we were particularly hungry, it was the short break in the routine of doing nothing that we craved! Breakfast, midmorning hot drinks, lunch, afternoon hot drinks, supper and even the last hot drink of the day all become major points of interest for any patient well enough to be bored. Some even anticipated the arrival of the drugs trolley baring medicines, tablets, the dreaded injections and even the totally embarrassing and degrading suppository! Strangely, though our bedside cupboards were bursting at the seams with snacks, fruit, sweets and a variety of soft drinks, it was the hot meals along with cups of free tea and coffee that captured our interest, if only for the entertainment value. So to actually refuse a hot drink within days of discharge was unheard of!

The tea lady tried again, 'What about a cold drink then? Squash or fruit juice?'

'No.'

'Coca cola?'

'No.'

'Just a glass of water then?'

'No thank you.'

'Well you really ought to drink something; you're still on a fluid chart you know!'

'No.'

'Ahh well, 'tis up to you. I bet you'd drink a pint of bitter though?'

'No. When I get home possibly but not now.'

At this the tea lady sighed in resignation and moved onto the next thirsty patient, me! No problems with me, I asked for two cups of tea in mugs if possible?

'No!' said the tea lady.

On sauntered the tea lady and her trolley companion, drifting throughout our bay giving satisfaction in the form of caffeine, chocolate or sugar to each eager patient before rattling the contraption out and into the next bay. Around me all the usual routines were now coming into play. Out came the packets of biscuits, slices of cake wrapped in tissue and brought from home, jaffa cakes, sweets and chocolate by the block. All the ingredients needed to make the simple cup of tea or coffee last longer and taste better. No one spoke as we munched happily on things we like but probably should not have, crumbs littering bed sheets and chocolate finger prints smeared down pyjamas. In silence all eyes were on the gent sprawled on in the bed adjacent to mine. 'Why didn't he want his drink? Was he unwell?' A silly question to ponder as he was in hospital; however we knew what we meant. The visitors then arrived with more biscuits, cake, chocolates and assorted nice things that we did not get when home, so we soon forgot the strange patient who did not want his drink.

An afternoon of chatter, opening packets, rustling papers and emptying of handbags was brought to an abrupt halt by the ringing of the bell that notified all that visiting time was over. Peace and quiet descended upon the ward as exhausted patients collapsed on their beds and tried to recover, ears still ringing from the inane gossip, news of relatives barely known and what little Johnny or Sharon had gotten up to at school. Snores, farts, coughs and shuffles were soon the only disturbances to break the blanket of silence, until the heated trolley containing our supper banged and crashed along the corridor outside the ward an hour or so later. We trained animals immediately awoke and began tidying our table surfaces, straightening our gaping pyjama bottoms and wiped our dribbling chins. Everyone on the ward readied themselves for the last monotony break of the day, even the guy next to me seemed keen to accept his evening meal, or so we thought.

Many people complain about hospital food, mostly because they have only ever known home cooking or highly priced restaurant food, and unrealistically expect their meals to have the same individual care and the same standard of menu they have long grown used to. Unfortunately hospitals have to supply food for huge numbers of individuals, thousands of patients and staff every day of the week. It is not logistically possible to cook each meal separately nor is it possible to cater for every single menu choice. Many moan about hospital fare, I am not one of these, I remember school meals! If the food is hot, on clean plates and has some semblance of taste then I am happy to eat it. I have never been a fussy eater, willing to try anything once. I do draw the line at squid, snails and raw celery but otherwise I will eat most things without qualm or vomiting. People who are regular inpatients like me, or those who have nourished their bodies with hospital food for days or weeks during their present incapacity soon develop a liking for this mass produced culinary delight. Those just arrived or short term patients do not seem able to share our acquired tastes. It quickly became suspect that the guy next to me whose name was George, was in the fussy category.

At last the enthusiastically awaited fest arrived, nurses and house keeping staff rallying around to ensure all patients received their meals as quickly and as hot as possible. No one was allowed to ring for a urine bottle or bed pan during this period, a case of cross your legs, clench your butt cheeks and eat as fast as you can! The meals were brought in individually and each patient closely examined the food presented to them, then they compared the meal received against the menu they had chosen the day before. This was done in an often futile attempt to identify what was on their plate and validate that it resembled its description! Meal choices were made by all on the previous day, by marking with a tick against each item listed that tempted your appetite. This card was then placed on a tray along with your meal, proof for all that you chose that menu so it was entirely your fault. I can never remember what I have ordered for my meals the preceding day; boredom having killed my brain long before a new day begins. So I too examined my meal and my little menu card on which I had ticked my preferred choice of culinary nourishment. Thoughts of '*Did I really ask for that? What the hell was I thinking?*' passed across my bewildered mind.

Mostly the results of the meal and menu examination followed this pattern; mistakes were rarely called to the attention of the nurses, unless some item had been accidently left off the meal tray. After all, we didn't want to starve! A lack of peas with our roast or no custard on our tart was enough to instigated shouts of;

'Nurse, I think I ordered . . . . .!'

Or 'Nurse, Where's my . . . . . ?'

Otherwise we all sat or lay and ate in silence, appreciating the simple acts of chewing, swallowing, gagging and disbelief when an item of food defied its description.

With the meal consumed, we all made ourselves comfortable on our beds and with sated bellies we sipped at cups of tea or coffee while wondering what we had ordered for tomorrow's lunch. It was not long before we all noticed that George next to me had not eaten a thing. His specially ordered bacon roll was lying cold and forlorn on its plate, no teeth marks evident on its limp crust. Sometimes, and only sometimes, when a patient is off their food and needs encouragement, the menu choice can be set aside and replaced with a favourite morsel such as a bacon roll. However the guy had not even glanced at it, he showed absolutely no interest in it, while we glared hungrily and wondered if we could creep over and steal it before the guy or the nurses noticed.

At the end of the meal distribution period, nurses went round each ward and patient to ensure all were satisfied and no one was having difficulties eating their meal. Although unsaid, the nurses were also checking no one had choked on a slice of gravy or a block of custard! It was a young student nurse that came in our ward and glanced around at all the discarded meal trays, checking how much each of us had eaten. Her gaze did not linger long on most of our plates because they had been licked clean. But then her soft brown eyes fell on the prone figure of George, then on his untouched meal tray upon which lay the now despondent bacon roll. With an almost imperceptible look of concern, the young nurse approached George and stood at his bedside.

'Hello there,' she said softly at first, just in case he was asleep and did not know his supper was rapidly decomposing on the little table beside him.

Upon receiving a grunt and opening of eyes, she continued, 'Did you not want your supper?'

'No,' replied the still prone George.

'What's up? I thought you liked bacon rolls?'

'I do but don't want it.'

'Not hungry?'

'No.'

'Have you eaten anything today?' enquired the yet unconcerned nurse.

'No.'

'What about drink? Have you had any drink today?'

'No.'

'Well you should be eating and drinking normally by now, you're due to go home soon. Would you like to try and eat some of your supper? Please?'

'No.'

Now the student nurse was concerned so off she went in search of a senior nurse to help with the situation. Moments later back she came with a stern looking companion.

'Why aren't you eating?' asked the staff nurse in a gentle voice, 'Can we get anything else to tempt you?'

'No.'

'Your daughter will be here soon, is she bringing anything in for you?'

'No I don't think so.'

'Well you must eat and drink something, How about a sip of water, just for me?' pleaded the staff nurse.

'No.'

'Just a small sip of water?'

'No thank you.'

The staff nurse had worked on the ward for some time, I had known her for years and I knew she would not let the matter rest. It was her job to look after we patients and she always took even the slightest concern as serious. Though still quite young it was obvious she knew her job well, and her instincts told her some underlying problems was stopped the guy from taking any form of nourishment.

'Can you tell me why you don't feel like eating?' she pleaded.

'Pills!' answered George.

'Pardon me? Pills? What do you mean?'

'Too many pills!'

'What's that got to do with you not eating?' she enquired, somewhat astonished.

'My belly is too full up with pills; I can't get any food in!'

'That's simply not true.' retorted the nurse while trying hard to remain polite.

By this time the attention of the whole ward was focused on this little scenario, I could not wait for the next instalment. George sat up in his bed, waggled a finger at the collection of empty little disposable tablet cups, and then looked sternly and in all sincerity at the two nurses standing beside his bed.

'Ever since I've been here you've been shoving pills down my throat, I've never had so many pills in my life! I haven't got any room left for food because I'm full of pills!'

Mouths gapped in bewilderment around the ward, even the nurses were shocked by this statement but I was empathic with the guy at this statement; often the huge amount of tablets and assorted medication funnelled into one when in hospital really took some consuming!

'Medication will not fill you up,' said the staff nurse, 'you only have a few each day and you need them in order to get better!'

'And they make me feel funny.'

'What do you mean; feel funny?'

'I feel all woolly in my head and I think it's those damn pills!'

'Maybe it's because you're not eating properly,' suggested the nurse, 'you need to take your tablets as well as eat and drink.'

'No.'

'Really you do, every patient in this hospital has to take their medicine while here, and you do need them.'

'No,' grunted George, 'you come round here four times a day will pills, surely twice a day would be enough? Don't need that many damn pills. Then you go and stick needles in me as well!'

'But you need your medication.' sighed the now frustrated staff nurse.

'No, don't want them.'

'And you won't get well if you don't eat.' interjected the student nurse.

'No, don't want them, don't want food, and don't want drink. I'm too full!' answered George with growing volume to his voice.

'How can you be full?' demanded the staff nurse, 'What about drink? Why haven't you been drinking?'

'I drink when I take those damn pills. That's enough, any more and I'll be peeing myself all day.'

'That's no reason why you shouldn't drink. What do you do at home? Do you manage to eat and drink OK at home?'

'Yes.'

'So what's different here?' asked the increasingly frustrated staff nurse.

'Pills!' was the short reply.

'Don't you take any tablets at home?'

'No.'

'Not ever?'

'No.'

'Well if you don't eat or drink you won't be allowed home. Do you want to go home?'

'No.' he replied but did not elucidate.

'So you want to stay here?' asked a surprised student nurse.

'No.'

Both nurses and all the other patients including myself stared open mouthed at this reply. So what did he want, was he nuts? Evening visiting time was fast approaching and both nurses were obviously very busy. However they continued to plead, beseech and beg the guy to take some sustenance, the tolerance and concern showed by the two nurses for this obviously disturbed guy was commendable. To each plea, every possible negotiation, every request they made, George's answer remained the same.

'No.'

Time passed and we fellow patients had become bored, none of us could believe the stubbornness of the guy, or the stupidity! Everyone one of us would have loved the attention he was getting, two attractive young nurses pleading at his bedside, using every ounce of their femininity to try and persuade him to eat and drink.

As visiting time became imminent, those of us expected or hoping for company tried to make ourselves look somewhat respectable, hiding urine bottles, bedpans, porn magazines, forbidden chocolate and other assorted items that may possible draw the wrath of spouses and siblings. Next to me the now somewhat annoying scene continued to run, both nurses pleading with a patient who continued to claim he was too full up with tablets to eat or drink.

At the allotted time, the corridor doors swung open in a rush, in poured people of every shape, size and age and carrying goodies and necessities as they rushed to the bedsides of those they had come to visit. On this night I was not expecting any visitors so I made ready to bury my head in a book, handheld computer card game or test my wits and ingenuity against the very modern patient personal television combined computer, radio and phone contraption. These devices are a new product of recent years and are supposed to allow the patient communication and entertainment while they rest in their beds awaiting recovery. The down side of these devices is that boredom drives patients towards them, either for the escape of television, the contact with friends via the internet or the sound of a loved ones voice on the telephone. I say downside because the cost of using these devices can often break a patient financially! The cost is frequently outweighed by the pressures of boredom and even loneliness, so patients ring their bank managers; request a second mortgage or cash loan, even an extension of their overdraft, just to allow two hours of television!

Seeing the visitors had arrived, the two nurses were forced to break off their verbal combat with George in order to avoid any possible disturbances to the ward as a whole. Promising to return they left the ward, leaving the pill saturated patient to flop down onto his pillow and resume his prone position. He had barely achieved this when a visitor arrived at his bedside. I assumed she was George's daughter but could not be sure of this at first. I did not want to appear rude so I turned away and attempted to ignore their quiet conversation. A moment or two passed before one of the nurses returned and indicated she would like to speak to the visitor in private, so both left the ward and closed themselves in the ward manager's office.

After a short time they both re-emerged and the visitor returned to George's bedside, a look of concern tinged with annoyance on her face. The visiting person was not unpleasant to look at, aged in her thirties I thought, well dressed with light brown wavy hair that reached her shoulders and a round face. Although not yet fat, it has to be said she was rather plump but still attractive in an ample sort of way.

'I hear you're not eating enough Dad?' she stated louder than before.

'No.'

'And why not? What's the matter? Is the food here not good enough?'

'Food seems OK.'

'Oh come on Dad, don't be silly. Why won't you eat anything?'

'I'm full up,' answered George.

'Yes; I've already been informed about your obsession that your medication is filling you up and ruining your appetite. That's just a load of rubbish. You can't be full up on pills; you'd need hundreds of them!'

'Seems like hundreds.'

'But it's not. No one takes hundreds of tablets, be sensible. How about I nip down to the hospital shop and pick you up something nice?'

'No thanks.'

'What about some Smarties then? You've always loved Smarties.'

'N . . er, yeah ok.'

'Gotcha!' shouted his daughter, 'Smarties are just like pills in shape and colour, so all you want is more tablets. Don't you?'

'No.'

'Now you're just being silly Dad, I'll get you some Smarties if you'll eat something else as well. Will you?'

'Dunno.'

'What do you mean, you don't know?'

'Dunno.'

'Oh I'm getting fed up with this! Are you going to eat something or not?'

'No.'

'Right, I'm off then Dad, I can't waste my time with you if you won't help yourself. I'll tell Mum that you're being daft. We'll see what she has to say.'

And with those angry parting words, George's daughter stormed out of the ward.

The poor guy was obviously quite upset by this exchange and it was then I realised there must be something truly amiss with him, maybe he was not just putting on an act in order to gain attention I wondered. George slipped down into his bed covers, curled up and closed his eyes, but not before I saw the hurt look on his face.

After visiting time had ended and the night staff had begun their shift, yet another nurse entered our ward and headed for George. She had been informed about his strange refusal to eat and was obviously intent on convincing him to take some form of nourishment. Before she reached him I signalled her over to me. Luckily it was one of the staff I knew quite well, she had worked on this ward for many years. Gesturing for her to draw nearer, I told her what had happened with his daughter and voiced my concerns that there could be a real problem here. She listened and considered what I had said, and then with a troubled look at George she left the ward. Moments later I could hear her talking on the phone to someone but could not catch what was said. George was allowed to sleep as no one came to pester him into eating again that night.

The next morning arrived at the ridiculous time of five thirty as the nurses rushed in to collect urine bottles, do the diabetic testing for those who needed it, jabbed needles into unsuspecting patients who suddenly became wide awake and to administer oral medication. By six thirty our ward had undergone all the necessary punishment and the nurses left us in peace to await breakfast. Most of us rolled over to snatch another hour's sleep, myself included. As I lay down and turned onto my side I could see George sitting up in bed looking anxiously at the door as if waiting for something. It was far too early in the day for my interest to arise, I ignored him and drifted off to my dream world of fame, fortune and pretty young nurses administering to my every wish, and I do mean every wish!

I awoke to the sound of the breakfast trolley entering the ward and accompanied by calls of; 'Good morning gentlemen. How are we today? Who wants breakfast? Keep it polite please gentlemen!' said Tyrone, a young man working as house keeper on this day.

'Hey mate,' called George, 'I haven't had my pills yet. Any chance you could find out what's happening please?'

'No problem George. I'll nip out and ask someone before I serve breakfast. If that's ok with you guys?'

'Nope!'

'Bugger off I'm hungry!'

'Not ok!'

'Feed me now!' was the assortment of replies.

'OK, I'll leave your breakfasts for a moment, seeing as you gentlemen are kind enough to wait.' then he left, before the first of several thrown slippers and one urine bottle could hit their target!

Within moments Tyrone was back again, followed closely by a senior staff nurse, looking very appealing in her crisp blue uniform, or at least she would have if we were not all still half asleep and staving to boot.

'What's up George?' she asked.

'I've not had all me pills yet. I normally have them early in the morning, I think they've forgotten me,' he answered pitifully.

'No it's fine. The doctor has stopped all you tablets for the time being. Instead we're going to give you an injection. That ok?'

'Bloody hell! An injection! What the hell for?'

'Well; the injection will give you all the medication you need without you having to take so many tablets. We know you don't like tablets.'

'So no more pills eh? Just one injection is it?'

'Yes, for now and we'll see how you manage today. Now then, are you hungry? Do you want some breakfast?'

'Damn right I do,' cried George, 'I'm bloody staving!'

'Tyrone,' called the nurse, 'can you make sure George has all that he wants for breakfast, plus two cups of drink please?'

'Don't tell me you're gonna eat today George? Dunno if I've got enough food for you as well,' replied Tyrone teasingly.

'You'd better have, otherwise I'll damn well eat you!'

'Okay, I'd best make sure you have a big breakfast then, I'm way too young to be eaten.'

'Leave some for us.'

'I'll eat you if you don't get a bloody move on.'

'Oi! Room service!'

'Come on, I'm starving here.'

Comments echoed from patients including some of the politer calls from around our ward as we all waited impatiently for breakfast to be served.

Throughout the day George happily ate his way through every scrap of food offered to him, he also consumed cups of tea by the bucket. Even his bedside cupboard was raided and the huge stack of previously unwanted snacks, chocolate, biscuits and sweets began to diminish briskly. George ate his way through that day, and much of the night judging by the constant crinkle and crack of various packets of biscuits and sweets being attacked in the dim light of the ward. The next morning George was up and about and obviously feeling fine, though not yet full it seemed. Once more he demolished his breakfast and I swear he even sized up some of the patients food with a hungry glint in his eye. We were given no explanation by George or anyone else as this abrupt change of behaviour, though most of us could throw in a good guess. George himself said nothing; he could not because his mouth was always full. With so much going in, it is a fact of nature that something must also come out. It was not long before George made almost as many trips to the toilet as he did to his food store!

Eventually the ward doctor came in to examine George and we all pricked up our ears to make certain we did not miss one single detail. George had become an item of pure interest.

'Well George, I see you've been eating again. How are you feeling today?' asked the doctor.

'I'm feeling much better thank you,' replied George.

'Well enough to go home?'

'Yep, certainly.'

'Ok then, I'll organise your discharge for later this morning. Is that ok? Do you have someone to pick you up?'

'I hope so. My daughter normally picks me up but I'll have to check she's forgiven me. I think I upset her a tad when she came to see me,' George sighed.

'Right; well let me know if you do require transport. Make sure you continue to eat and we'll set out instructions for you to visit your local GP each for your injection, at least until you are properly better. How does that sound?'

'That's fine doctor, thank you very much. One question though, was it the pills that stopped me eating?'

'We're not totally sure George, it may have been that because you believed the medication made you lose your appetite, your body responded and suppressed your hunger. That's the only explanation we can give at the moment, it is biologically impossible to become full on just a hand full of tablets.'

'Ahh, right,' said George with a knowing expression on his face. 'Thank you again doctor, I'll ring my daughter now and take the ear bashing.'

The doctor had barely left the ward before George began muttering to himself loudly. Getting up from his bed, George left the ward to hunt down a telephone he could use to contact his daughter. Some time later he returned, looking relieved and headed towards his bed to get dressed behind the drawn curtains. It was nice to see George well enough to be discharged, better still to see him go before he began munching his way through our own food supplies. When dressed and packed, George looked as each of us and wished us all good luck and a fast recovery, but just before departing our four walled world he suddenly turned back to us and grinned.

'See? I told them bloody doctors it was the pills filling me up. All this psycho rubbish about it being in me head, never heard so much tripe. Who do they think I am? Am I some kind of fool who don't know the difference between thinking something and feeling something? I don't think so. I know it was all those damn pills they were chucking in me, it's not in me head, t'was in me belly. Silly buggers!'

And with that all compromising statement, George left the ward and headed off to meet his forgiving daughter. We each had our own ideas on the root cause of George's failure to eat. Most considered the explanation giving by the doctor to be the correct one; it was all in George's mind. After all he was the qualified doctor and he would not say something that was not true, would he? Personally I felt George had a point also, he may have been nearer the mark than the others gave him credit for. George had been full up on pills!

Chapter Six: The Lost Slippers.

Confusion is often rampant on the average hospital ward, a mixture of illness, injury, medication and strange surroundings can play tricks on the mind. Mind tricks that seldom affect us in the familiar environment of our own homes. However when people find themselves in hospital, it can be very difficult for many to distinguish between drugs or sickness induced hallucinations, simple mind tricks or actual real events. Lost in a strange medical world, populated with stranger people and working routines that often defy logic. So when a new patient begins demonstrating signs of abnormal or simply weird behaviour, the more regular patients look on in amusement and anticipation of the show set to gain centre stage. The more experienced staff watch with resignation, they have seen it all before.

Such an event revelled itself upon the arrival of one new patient. Quite an elderly chap; tall, very thin and obviously quite ill. Once admitted and settled into his bed in the corner of the ward nearest the doors, the guy introduced himself as Archie and announced politely that he was pleased to meet us, but wished it were under better circumstances. He informed us this was his first time as a patient in hospital, but he hoped he would not be in too long. He seemed a nice chap, but I felt something was amiss; something was not quite right with Archie. When new patients first come onto a ward, they are normally silent, frightened and lonely. It is common for a new patient not to engage in conversation with other patients for several hours or even days! Encountering an older gent who immediately introduced himself signified either he was very used to hospital admissions, which we knew he was not, or we had a show in the offering.

A nurse duly arrived and began recording Archie's details, logging each one onto a file that would eventually be added to his complete medical records for future doctors to ignore. Blood pressure, temperature, blood oxygen levels and list of his present medication were meticulously noted down. Diet and next of kin followed along with mobility skills and his normal standard of health. Finally the last piece of information was required and the nurse pulled out a photocopied list with accompanying sketched pictures. We all knew what information was sought and to be honest, none of we fellow patients gave the question much importance, but the new guy did!

'One last thing I need Archie,' reeled off the nurse automatically, 'What are your bowels like?'

'What?' exclaimed Archie in surprise.

A look of pure confusion mingled with horror flew across his face! Nervously he glanced about himself and the ward, looking first at us, then at his lower waist, then at the nurse and back to his waist.

'What do you want to see my bowels for?'

Archie gave a stern look to the nurse, who like many of the nursing staff in this hospital was young and very attractive, whereas Archie was of pensioner age and apparently a gentleman of the old school.

'It's OK; I only need to know if your bowels are working correctly. I don't need to actually see them. Are you opening your bowels regularly? Daily, every couple of days or are you having some problems?' concluded the nurse in a resigned but understanding tone.

Again Archie looked terrified, peering round at each of us in bewilderment and an evident lack of understanding. At this point realisation hit me! I knew what the poor guy was thinking and I decided to help out in a manner he may be more accustomed to.

'Hey; Archie!' I called across the ward, 'What she means is do you have a crap every day, a few times a week or are you bound up like a stuffed turkey?'

Relief flooded Archie's face, relief and some embarrassment.

'No; no I go every day. Nothing wrong with me down there,' he almost shouted as he realised his fears were unfounded.

With a discreet grin the nurse then showed Archie the sheet containing written descriptions and pictures.

'Can you indicate what your normal stools look like please?' she enquired gently.

Archie pointed at one of the sketches and muttered shyly that picture was a similar representation. After this final piece of information, the nurse suggested he readied himself for examination by a doctor in the next hour or so, and then she left, throwing me a dazzling smile as she went.

'Thank goodness for that!' sighed Archie to the ward as a whole, 'I thought she wanted to examine my butt. You know the finger up the back passage routine. I really didn't want a young filly prodding my bum; it would have been too embarrassing.'

We laughed along with him at this admission; he was obviously more of a gentleman than the rest of us. The majority of we male patients would have secretly relished the prospect of being hidden behind the bed curtains while a pretty young nurse prodded us. Again, hospital boredom does not always bring out the best in a patient.

This was not the only entertainment Archie provided during his stay on our ward. It seems he had another oddity that had not come to light yet. The next instalment of his side show was to materialise later that evening. It was just past nine and all the day staff and visitors had gone, we had gratefully accepted our last hot drink of the day and now just awaited the medication trolley. I have never understood why we were served a hot drink at about eight thirty but our medication did not appear until after nine. Surely it would have made sense to dish out the tablets, medicines, laxatives, uppers; downers, strange brews and knockout pills along with a hot drink? Alas this is not feasible on a busy hospital ward, the nurses undertake each chore as and when the situation allows, one cannot place the importance of a drink above the medical needs of patients.

This time in the evening was normally quiet, many of the older patients were already fast asleep, heads tilted back on their pillows, false teeth hanging loose from their mouths and a small trickle of spittle making its way in a narrow line down their chins. The younger patients or those, like me who did not sleep too well, were busy reading books, concentrating over crossword puzzles, listening to the radio or attempting to find the one programme that might appeal amongst the multiple channels of rubbish found on the bedside patient televisions. Personally I always used this time to check and answer my emails, a long and laborious task on these strange bedside devices but at least I could keep in touch with friends and family. This act always puzzled the older patients in the ward, most had no idea how one could use the internet, never mind using it from a television! I gave up trying to explain several years ago.

Most of the patients were now in pyjamas and were in or lying on their beds. Archie had settled in very well after his little scare earlier and he too was laying reading on his bed. The medication duly arrived and we feasted on the multicoloured results of scientific wisdom, and winced at needles pushed into various parts of our bodies. After this the main ward lights were extinguished and those who chose to, switched on their dim bed side lamps to continue their efforts to find entertainment during the dark hours. This time also instigated the toilet run, each patient apparently being overcome with the desire to relieve bladders before attempting to sleep in the stuffy heat and noise of the hospital night.

Archie had not turned his light on, obviously intending to sleep after taking his short trip to the toilet. Off the bed he rose, slid his feet into his slippers and ventured off to his ablutions. This was the first time Archie had clambered from the sanctity of his bed since joining our little band of brothers, which may have included uncles, fathers and transvestites. The chore concluded, Archie returned satisfied to his bed and climbed in, pulled the covers up to his ears and within moments had joined the cacophony of snores that were now echoing round the ward. I and one other patient kept our lights on, I was still fighting to answer emails while the other chap fought with crossword or sudoku puzzles in a daily newspaper.

At ten o'clock I signed off the internet and began searching for a suitable film, hoping it would be a long one and I would not have to face the dreaded prospect of attempting sleep too soon. The scratching of a pen on paper told me the other patient was also still awake. The snores, farts, grunts and groans informed me the other four other patients in the ward were all asleep. Outside the ward the nurses settled down at the desk for a quick break, no bells were buzzing, no patients were shouting for a relative long since passed away, and no confused patients were wandering the corridors like spectres in the night. I had found a film, Rambo I think, and alternated between watching the film I had seen many times before, and chomping on biscuits and other assorted snacks. The pen still scratched in the darkness across the ward.

Just as the film finished, the next round of toilet runs began. Older people seldom sleep right through a night without waking once or twice to empty a bladder shrunken with age. I was no different; all my life I have been a hopeless sleeper but now I had become a frequent loo traveller as well. One by one over a period of 30 minutes or so, each patient woke and made the short trip to the toilet which was situated immediately outside the bay doors. I successfully made my first trip of the night, knowing that I would need to retrace my steps more than once this night, along with the biscuits I had also been sipping at a drink near to hand on my bedside table. My fault I know, but what else was there to do except eat, drink and watch old films? Last to visit the toilet was Archie, sleep still trying to bind his eyes, and tired muscles striving to obtain more rest. His duty done, Archie return to his bed and was soon asleep once more.

At last I too drifted off to sleep some two hours later following a couple of chapters of my book and lots of restless tossing and turning. I must have only been asleep a few moments before I was woken by the grating sound of the nurse call buzzer. Who the hell has pressed their bell I wondered, as far as I knew, all occupying the ward were able bodied and capable of sorting themselves out. With a few nasty thoughts about patients and their bells, I closed my eyes and tried to drift off into unconsciousness for the second time. No such luck!

'Who's ringing?' enquired a soft voice from the doorway.

'Me.'

'Who's me?'

'It's me, Archie.'

'What do you what Archie, can't you sleep?'

'No it's not that, I want the toilet but I can't find my slippers. Can you help me please?'

The nurse agreed and before long both she and Archie were peering around his bed in the gloom.

'Here they are,' said the nurse while bending to retrieve the elusive footwear. 'They're over this side of the bed.'

'Dunno how they got there,' Archie replied, 'I always leave my slippers on the same side of the bed.'

Archie then thanked the nurse who went back to her station and Archie headed for the toilet. Peace reasserted itself and I nodded off to sleep once more with no more disturbances that night.

The next day passed in complete and utter monotony, the only highlights being the usual meal times and the antics of the over whelmed visitor. No one was discharged from our ward so no new patients trespassed into our little world. Evening arrived as it always does, following the day, and as routine demanded we all set about getting ourselves prepared for the night. By nine o'clock all hot drinks had been served, all medication administered and silence reigned while chaos had a holiday.

Around ten o'clock the main lights were turned off and the usual two bedside lamps cast shadows across the floor, my own and that of the scribbler as he continued to tackle more newspaper puzzles. Most of the other patients had already completed the toilet run and bedclothes were arranged, teeth, hearing aids and wigs were removed, newspapers and books were closed and the ward readied itself for the nightly onslaught of snores, farts, rumbles, groans, burps and various other outlets of sound, wind and odours.

Archie was again the last of the four sleepers to make the loo trip as he had already been dozing heavily for much of the evening. Throwing back the covers, he draped his legs over the side of his bed and his toes wriggled as he searched for his slippers again. With a loud sigh of frustration he stood up and closely examined the floor area beside the bed.

'Where the *hell* are my slippers this time?' he muttered angrily.

I looked over along with the only other patient remaining awake, the pen scratcher, whose bed was next to Archie's. In the faint light from pen scratcher's bedside lamp I could just make out the shape of his slippers.

'They're on the other side of the bed Archie,' I said.

'What are they doing over there? I didn't put them there.' muttered Archie as he pottered round his bed to collect his slippers.

'I hope none of you buggers are playing tricks on me?' he said with only a trace of humour.

The pen scratcher and I both assured him we had not been messing with his slippers and had no idea how they had gotten to the opposite side of the bed.

'What side of the bed do you leave your slippers at home Archie?' the pen scratcher suddenly asked.

'On the left side. Wife sleeps on the right side so I can't get in or out that side, she's too big to climb over and I'd hate for her to get the wrong impression if she awoke and caught me straddling her in the middle of the night!'

Slippers on his feet, Archie toileted and climbed back into bed, still muttering about wandering slippers. Later that night, with emails completed and the late night film watched, I had just picked up my book when Archie arose once again for the toilet. The same procedure began. First he sat up in bed and swung his legs over the side, his feet then searched for his slippers but alas in vain once more. Again they appeared to have disappeared. With angry mutterings and some really choice words I would not have expected from a gentleman, Archie moved towards the nurse call button and was about to jab a bony finger against the illuminated button that we all joked would make a nurse come!

'Archie,' I whispered as loud as possible, many older people cannot hear too well and Archie was no exception. 'They're on the other side of the bed again.'

Archie threw his hands into the air in exasperation, 'Again? What the hell is going on here?'

Marching round to the other side, he slammed his feet in the slippers and stomped off to the toilet. A few minutes later he returned, quieter now. I watched him as he walked over to the left side of his bed and clambered in, just like he did at home. I noticed the pen scratcher was also watching Archie's antics, but with raised eyebrows and amusement on his face.

'You still awake Archie?' the pen scratcher asked quietly a moment later.

'Yes; why what's the matter?'

'I think you dropped something when you came back in.'

'No I don't think so, I wasn't carrying anything,' retorted Archie.

'Well something dropped,' insisted the pen scratcher, 'Perhaps you should just check?'

With a heavy sigh Archie again sat up and swung his legs over the side of the bed.

'Stop!' called the pen scratcher.

Archie stopped mid swing, 'Why?' he asked.

'What side of the bed are you getting out?'

Archie threw the pen scratcher an annoyed look, 'This side of course! It's nearest to the door.'

'What side is that?'

'It's the right side . . . . . . Oh!

'Yep that's right,' grinned the pen scratcher, 'You leave your slippers and get into bed on this side, your left side, but when you get out for the toilet you get out the right side because, as you said, it's nearer!'

'Oh, er, umm,' stammered Archie.

'That's why your slippers seem to move. You're getting into bed on the left, but getting out of bed on your right. Your slippers remain on the left.'

'Oh bugger!' said Archie.

I had watched and listened to this latest instalment of hospital capers and chuckled quietly into my bed sheets. The nurse came into the ward to see what all the noise was about and poor old Archie had to explain and apologise to her for his behaviour. Red faced, Archie had to tolerate the muted guffaws of laughter from the nurse, myself and the pen scratcher.

The next day Archie attempted to explain his odd antics. It appeared that at home he did in fact get in and out of the left side of his bed as his wife slept on the right hand side. Here in hospital he still got into bed on the left side, but as he already explained, the door from the ward and the toilet outside were on the right of his bed. Without thinking he had been taking the shortest route, forgetting he had placed his slippers on the floor beside the left of his bed.

And so the problem of the lost slippers was solved. To the relief of Archie!

But it was the pen scratcher who had the last words as with a cheeky grin he called across to Archie.

'Hey Archie, have you ever been to a real tailor?'

'Yes why?'

''Well I hope you remembered your left from right when the tailor asked '*What side does Sir dress on?*', after all, you don't want to lose that!'

Chapter Seven: Windy Julie

Obviously not all humorous stories originate solely in the male wards of a hospital but alas I am not privileged to give accounts on life in the female ward for some strange reason. Interesting events can happen in every ward or department just as they would in any normal work place or venue where people gather. Restaurants are known for the strange and funny behaviour of their clients, factories all have a joker in their midst. Offices and large retail stores also have odd occurrences and events that present humour to the onlooker. Even Parliament has its comedian, though he/she is mostly known by the title of Chancellor! Hospital wards are no different, geriatric or children's ward, male or female, all have a tale to tell.

This story was passed on to me by a female friend who also enjoyed frequent visits to her local medical hostelry. One may assume female wards would be politer and quieter than the male equivalent, but in truth this is not the case. When women gather together they can be just as raucous and coarse as any group of males, sometimes more so. Women tend to act more naturally towards each other when no males are present, where as men continue to compete with each other and retain a defence of their true feelings especially towards other males. This can mean that when women let loose, they let loose totally and in style!

My friend called Julie was incarcerated in a ward containing five other female patients, making six in total and all had been admitted for the same health reasons. Julie is a shy soft spoken woman with blond hair and fair complexion. She was in her late thirties to early forties and slim figured. Julie had been admitted into hospital for a hysterectomy as had all the other women in the ward. The National

Health Service was attempting to beat cuts in government funding by operating in bulk, a production line of hysterectomies in one sweep.

The other women in the ward ranged in ages, sizes and shapes. Large women and thin women, tall and short, women aged in their twenties up to those in their fifties. Each one had been taken to the operating theatre on the same day and admitted onto the ward within hours of each other. As is often the case, as soon as full consciousness had been regained, each of the women introduced themselves and began relating the experiences of their individual operations along with the reasons why they had chosen this form of surgery. Several it seemed had decided to undergo the procedure to avoid the possibility of falling pregnant with more children. Again the raison d'être behind this appeared to be different for each of the women. Some had several children and did not want more, feeling they had done enough damage to the human race already by bringing such little hooligans into the world. One did not want children under any circumstances, she wanted to retain her sanity and the remainder were having the hysterectomy for health issues. Whatever the motive behind the operation, all felt a form of companionship with the others as they had each been through the same procedure and experience of a National Health *Slice & Dice!*

Soreness and discomfort accompanied each patient following their unconscious removal from the theatre and short journey into the ward, so it was not until the next day that most felt up to much movement. Some of the patients had drains attached in order to allow any excess fluids to drain away harmlessly, all had catheters fitted as toileting can be difficult after such a procedure. A long uncomfortable night filled with moans, groans and sharp curses followed the medical measures. The women turned in their sleep, only to be awoken by stabbing pains as a result of their wounds, drains or catheters left each one tired and unsure of what the next day would bring. All of the women had an intravenous drip attached to their arms that administered a pain killer to help reduce the discomfort but the occasional sharp pain still managed to get through, often resulting in screaming, cursing and hollering.

As the new day grew into fullness, a few catheters were removed from those recovered enough and the patients were encouraged to get up and move around carefully. Others needed longer to recover sufficiently depending on which procedure they had along with their health and age. It was Julie who first to noticed an increasing pain in her abdomen and mentioned it to the other patients. She was surprised by the replies that quickly indicated the others were feeling the same! When one of the nurses came into the ward, Julie sought advice.

'Excuse me,' said Julie, 'I have some pain that seems to be getting worse in my lower stomach, any ideas on what's causing it? All the others are feeling the same.'

'Oh that's nothing, in fact it's to be expected,' replied the nurse with a smile. 'It's only a bit of wind my dear. It's nothing to worry about.'

'Are you sure? It seems more painful than just friggin' wind.'

'Yes of course dear, it happens all the time.'

'Why? Isn't it enough that the operation was painful, now we have to be blown up like those sex dolls the dirty old men use?'

'Now don't be crude Miss, I know what you mean but wind is a by product of your hysterectomy, which ever type of procedure you had.'

'Huh?' asked a puzzled Julie.

'Well my dear, if you had what's known as keyhole surgery; they pump some carbon dioxide into you to blow things up a bit so they can see inside you easily. That gas has to go somewhere and you may find you'll start getting some indigestion pains until the gas is absorbed or expelled by your body.'

'Oh lovely!' exclaimed another patient, 'CO_2 floating around inside us. How long before it gets out and pollutes the atmosphere?'

'Don't be silly dear,' sighed the nurse.

'Silly? There are six of us in here, that's a lot of gas!'

'What are the other types or kinds of hysterectomy then?' Julie enquired before the other patient exploded, literally!

'There are several other forms but I think you're referring to the cause of your trapped wind?'

'Yep!' said Julie.

'Too bloody true,' muttered one of the other patients.

'Ahh well; when you have someone messing around with your internals, your body, er . . .; sort of shuts down for a while. So any wind you may have in your system can't get out until your bowels begin functioning properly again. That's all, nothing to worry about.'

'Unless you're also constipated!' quipped one of other patients.

Apparently this brief explanation was all we were going to get and the nurse then had to leave the bay to answer a call bell in an adjoining ward. Though this information did not help the patients to feel better, it did ease their concerns slightly. For the rest of the morning the ward and its inhabitants continued as normal, a wash and bed tidying followed by a small group of young doctors, mostly male for some reason, examining each patient. The mid morning tea trolley arrived, a welcome sight to all the patients after a previous day of starvation and being trussed and prodded in the operating theatre. This brief interlude of excitement over, the patients settled down to rest.

Their bodies were still sore and pain continued to be constant, even with the painkilling drugs slowly dripping into their arms via a long plastic needle.

Lunch came and went, those could eat did and those who could not yet face hospital food settled for a cup of tea and a biscuit or toast. Visitors arrived, mostly worried looking husbands or partners, some with screaming hordes of children in tow and faces portraying the pleasure of looking after these little angels at home by themselves. Conversations rippled around the room before sinking into quieter tones as each husband or partner received the next set of instructions on chores to be done and shopping to buy. During this exchange the most common phrases to be heard were lists of chores and matters that required attention.

'Yes dear' or 'No dear,' were the constant replies.

When the visiting period had run its course and with the sound of the bell signifying its end, sighs of quiet relief could be heard from both patients and visitors alike. The male counterparts heading off once more to the turmoil known as home, the patients settling down to rest following a stressful time of pacifying children and reassuring husbands or partners.

Julie was ashamed for berating her husband forcefully when he admitted to confusing the children's supper with the dog food, sending their son off to school in his sister's knickers and not knowing which cupboard contained the vacuum cleaner. But that was not the only reason she was grateful visiting time had concluded. Julie was bursting with wind! The pain in her stomach and the urge for relief were almost unbearable. Finally nature overcame good manners and Julie broke wind with a rumble that reverberated round the ward.

'I'm so sorry,' said Julie apologetically, 'It must be what that nurse was talking about. I just couldn't hold it in any longer.'

She need not have worried; barely had her words left her lips when several more loud rumbles rocked the room.

'I'm sorry too,' said one of the patients,

'Me too!' said another.

'Yep and me,' said a third.

Suddenly the room resounded to the sound of feminine giggles intermixed with explosions of released gas. It soon became evident that Julie was not the only sufferer in the ward, each of the other patients had been desperately holding themselves back in case they offended those around them. But now the cat was out of the bag, or rather the cat had been blown out of the bag, as one by one the patients sought relief through the expelling of trapped wind. Julie and her fellow patients were too sensible to worry about manners at a time like this. Everyone now understood the reasons for such released gales and with an unspoken agreement; each patient continued farting happily upon desire. The tempest continued throughout the remainder of the day and only halted when evening visiting time arrived once more. It has to be said that some visitor's expressions proved interesting when they entered the ward, but in true British style, not one commented on the strange aroma that hung in the air.

Gradually as the last visitor departed with the sound of the bell ringing in their ears, the crescendo of noise built up once more in the ward. Farting! Often in unison accompanied by giggles and chatter turned quickly into laughter as the patients bonded through mutual experience and good humour. The nurse shifts had changed and the night nurses were now in sole control of the wards. Silence had reigned when they had come on duty as the visitors were still present on the wards so they had no warning of the sudden uproar and strange noises that emitted from Julie's ward. Until the visitors left!

'What is going on in here?' said one of the night nurses as she rushed into the room.

'We're expressing ourselves,' said one of the patients.

'What do you mean, expressing yourselves? How are you expressing yourselves as you call it?' demanded the nurse who was convinced they were mocking her.

She should not have asked. Almost in synchronization, mighty blasts of escaping wind answered her question. Laughter followed the last explosion, driving the poor nurse from the room in horror! Some moments later she returned with backup, the senior staff nurse had been recruited to help with the situation. The staff nurse wrinkled her nose as she entered the room, paused and looked round at each patient.

'How many of you have had a hysterectomy?' she asked.

'All of us,' answered one of the patients.

'Thought so,' she muttered, 'well; please keep the verbal noise down at least, even if you can't control the other noises at the moment.'

With a knowledgeable smile at her colleague, the staff nurse left the ward with the junior nurse hastening in her wake. Julie and the other patients duly muted their conversation and laughs so the rest of the evening passed uneventfully though still quite aromatic.

The next day saw a vast improvement in many of the patients, resulting in the ward doctors pondering on the rapid recovery. The rumbling gales had slowly decreased as bodies and bowels returned to normal. After the explosive cessation of prudence and what is normally deemed as good manners, the laughter that ensued created an atmosphere of companionship amongst the six patients. Stresses and worries failed to drag the patients down and with the aid of peer encouragement, recovery continued at an unusually fast rate. Over the next few days the patients health and ability increased so well that Julie and one other were discharged two days earlier than normal, other patients being sent home on or a day before the established time period had expired.

The nurses gently explained to the baffled doctors that a happy ward often led to quick recoveries and Julie's ward had been one of the jolliest they had seen in a long time. When the doctors enquired why this particular ward was so cheerful, a nurse informed them it was all down to wind! Enjoying the puzzled expression on the doctor's face, the mischievous nurse decided not to enlighten them further. In her opinion after years in college then university and on into medical school and all the training it took to be a doctor, they would figure it out for themselves, eventually. Finally when the last patient on Julie's ward had been discharged, there followed a frantic period of opening windows and cleaners armed with cans of air fresher before the next intake of patients arrived.

And all because the lady loved – to break wind!

Chapter Eight: Visitors.

It is not just the patients that provide amusement in hospitals; the visitors can be just as interesting, sometimes even hilarious! You only have to find a quiet secluded seat somewhere amidst the hustle and bustle of the day to day hospital rush and routine, and watch the story of human evolution unfold before your eyes.

Visitors obviously come in all shapes and sizes, all creeds and all ages, but the majority of these by far are elderly female friends or relatives of elderly relatives or friends who are inpatients within the medical establishment. The musky smell of mothballs permeates the air and strange time defying hats and scarves adorn gray or blue rinse heads. Handbags and walking sticks clenched tightly, held in readiness to defend against any misfortunate miscreant that may cross their path. The fragrance of huge bunches of flowers competing with the over powering smell of perfume wafts through corridors, waiting rooms and toilets; baring witness to the arrival of the senior visitor. Buxom women can be seen charging purposefully along the corridors, often with a frail worn out husband trailing in their slipstream. Small, wizened and fragile old ladies with iron wills gather in packs of two or three and wander haphazardly along corridors, forcing all before them to move out of the way. Hobbling patients, those in wheelchairs or being transported from ward to ward via their hospital bed are no exception. Doctors, nurses and other visitors are unceremoniously pushed aside as the hunting pack of ancient women meander along, chatting incessantly; all are expected to give way to the venerable long term denizens of the world.

Elderly gentlemen appear to treat the task of visiting a relative or friend in hospital as the ultimate challenge. They march with apparent confidence along corridors and into wards, desperately trying to exude health and strength in the face of such human suffering. Only to quickly eject themselves as they realise their old friend and army buddy is unlikely to be found on the maternity ward! Glancing neither left nor right and asking no one for help, they stride out once more, gifts, papers or flowers grasped securely in one hand, the other swinging in perfect time to their footsteps. These self assured gentlemen eventually arrive at their intended destination, often after miles walked in wrong directions along endless corridors, finally stepping as lively as possible up to the recipient of their visit. However when asked how they had found the ward and if they had experienced any difficulties, the reply is always the same.

'No; no trouble at all. I know my way around; I've travelled the world y'know. I found my way straight to you in no time at all.'

Another type of elderly gentleman visitor could not be so opposite. Thin, unhealthy and frightened looking men shuffle slowly along the corridors, looking more like patients than visitors. Stepping aside for each and every person who enters their proximity and nodding politely with a smile as they linger in corners or alcoves while the all too fast population rushes by.

Unlike the proud ex-forces gentlemen, these elderly males are only too happy to receive assistance, smiling pitifully at the young nurses as they pass by in their crisp and appealing uniforms. Unfortunately for these poor individuals, it is normally one of the forceful matronly visitors who steps up to the challenge and offers to guide him on his way. Happy that someone else has accepted the responsibility but secretly disappointed it was not offered by someone younger, sexier and softer featured.

Speaking only for the older or mature male, the ability to chase or attract the young shapely female may have long diminished, but just like noticing a superior painting or beautiful landscape view, the sight of a young attractive woman will still stir interest, not a lot it must be said. It is sadly the age and inclination of body parts that restrict further pursuit of the fair young maiden! The timid gentlemen crave assistance where ever they are, in hospitals, supermarkets or libraries, they all seek a leader. Sadly it is often those single individuals who live alone and see all too few people on a daily basis, reflecting the opposite situation; these mild mannered men can also be the result of a long and obedient marriage. After many decades of being married to the same person, these gentlemen have long since lost the ability to think for themselves and also rely on others to take control, especially forceful women.

Younger males enter the hospital with secret desires of finding a pretty and willing young nurse, while young women search for that young handsome doctor on which to apply their charms.

Other species of visitor create different problems to staff and patients alike. In fact in my experience I would state that this group of visitors are dreaded by all those working or recovering in hospital. The family group! Often consisting of three or four generations and each one intent on being heard above the rest, children vying for attention and grandparents complaining about their own health and woes. Fathers trying desperately to appear in control but in reality remain invisible to mothers, wives and daughters. A medical environment is largely unimportant to young boys as the big adventure playground formally known as a hospital fills their heads with excitement and curiosity. Male teenagers with heads hidden under hoods, ears plugged with IPods, hands stuffed deeply into pockets and shoulders hunched. A carefully crafted sullen expression on their faces as they strive to show the world their boredom and reluctance to be in such an un-cool building, while at the same time trying to distance themselves from their family around them. Daughters, sisters and even aunties shuffle along with heads bowed over mobile phones, their thumbs moving in a blur as endless text messages leap frantically into the ether and speed to the recipient, yet another young person with their head bowed over a mobile phone.

When the family group appear on the ward, everyone sighs with resignation. Mothers and fathers leading the family group as grannies, in-laws, assorted other relatives and tribes of young and hyperactive kids invade the ward. Totally ignoring the many and prominent signs that state only two visitors per bedside, this unruly bunch of noise polluters assault the ward and everyone's space. Descending on their chosen victim, some poor family member who would rather be left in peace, they drag chairs into place and a circus ensues. With each adult seated, a mother will vainly attempt to restrain those lovely innocent little children that cannot by law be punished. Thanks to *do-gooders* in modern society who have never had children, or if they had, a nanny would have dealt with the terrible two's and the ferocious four's, right up to the terrifying teens.

Once gathered like Native Americans surrounding the European immigrants or first generation white American wagon train in a black and white movie, the patient is surrounded. Any progress in recovery is now brought to an abrupt halt. The patient's senses quickly become overwhelmed as the adults all talk at once in loud voices. The children bored in seconds, soon begin to climb on, over and under the bed, open bedside cupboards, drink the squash brought in by another, more acceptable visitor earlier in the day, eat the grapes and leave shoe marks on the bed sheets. The patient smiles wanly, trying hard to appear grateful that so many of his family love him enough to visit him in his hour of need. He interjects where he can when an infrequent gap opens in the tirade of verbal compost emitted by his visitors, but no one seems to hear, or care.

Bored by the limited surroundings of the sick relative, the children eventually notice the huge variety of curiosities, shiny objects, unopened cupboards and potential victims within the ward. With shouts of glee, the dear little children begin terrorising any stranded patient who is unlucky enough not to have his own visitors to protect him! Urine bottles, bedpans, curtain screens, and bedside tables all disappear in the youthful whirlwind, emerging as flying objects moments later. Races are held between the children up and down the ward, walking frames, canes and any other available appliances all being incorporated as each attempts to conquer their siblings. Snotty, red faces appear beside the beds of patients, questions ripping out of food encrusted mouths while fingers explore green smeared nostrils.

'Hey mister, what's wrong with you?'

'What's that for?'

'What does this machine do?'

'What will happen if I switch it off? Will you die?'

'Can I have one of your sweets?'

'Why haven't you got someone to see you?'

'Gimme a biscuit mate?'

'Got any chocolate Mister?'

And on and on until more loud voices join the fray, this time from the parents and grandparents, as they pretend to care what the produce of their loins are up to.

'Johnny! Put that down!'

Johnny does not listen.

'Stevie, don't pull out that plug!'

Stevie does not listen.

'Robert! Stop bouncing on that gentleman's bed!'

Robert does not listen.

Long after chaos has turned both ward and patients upside down, one brave adult will lose their temper and wade in amongst the children. Then with many threats, jerked collars and grabbed wrists, the children are rounded into a small herd and forced to return to the corral of the family, for a few minutes before the whole scenario repeats once again.

Not all visitors are so raucous. Unfortunately all too often the vision of a wife, husband or partner sitting silently beside the bed that contains a very sick loved one can strike compassion in even the hardest soul. Sitting in mute observation, periodically reaching out to gently straighten a bed cover or stroke their partners hand or brow. The patient lies unconscious on the bed, their body desperately trying to repair itself while remaining sadly unaware of the tenderness portrayed by the figure sitting alongside them. A cough or muttered word, a small movement or intake of breath will bring a rapid response from the sentinel, before a slight falling of shoulders or a soft sigh signals there has been no change, the patient still lays prone and oblivious. Sometimes a small tear will form in the watchers eye, a discreet sob or wringing of hands will indicate the hidden turmoil raging inside. Small talk, a one sided whispered conversation may ensue as the visitor speaks gently to the still figure on the bed, hoping that some words may penetrate the sleeping mind and confirm the deep felt affection between them. When visiting time concludes and the lonely figure rises to leave, a soft kiss is left to linger on the patient's forehead, a parting gift of love given in hope to the unconscious and unaware partner.

Care and affection is commonly shown in other ways when a loved one is interned in hospital. One of the frequent forms of visitor is the wife and grown daughter together faithfully visiting a husband and father. The scenario always seems to follow the same format. In strides the wife followed closely by the daughter, acquiring chairs as they make purposefully towards the object of their visit. There is no uncertainty, no hesitation or reluctance in their movements as they position themselves each side of the patient's bed. Once seated the pair promote themselves to a position of carer and begin their administrations over the poor defenceless male. First the wife will unceremoniously empty his bedside cupboard, dragging out used pyjamas and underwear and piling on the bed for the world to see. The daughter then sorts out the soiled clothing and places it into a plastic bag in readiness for transport home and the washing machine. The daughter then moves away from the bed so the wife can screen off the patient by drawing the curtain round the bed. The husband is then stripped of any remaining item of clothing by his wife and squeezed into crisp and clean issues. With a violent swish the curtains are drawn back even as the patient is struggling into the clean pyjama bottoms. Swiftly the daughter swoops up the discarded clothing and that too is stuffed into the bag.

Next the bed itself falls under their attention, pillows are fluffed up and sheets are pulled and straightened, covers smoothed and when all reaches the required standard, covers and sheets are forcefully tuck in around the bed. All this activity has whirled about the bemused patient, a look of resignation upon his face. He has said nothing while the two women fussed and chattered over him, asking questions and answering them before he can even decide upon a reply, pushing and manoeuvring him round the bed like a sack of potatoes, and giving him the same amount of dignity as one would give potatoes. Food and drink carefully arranged for his satisfaction gains their attention next, each item being picked up, examined and placed in to a more suitable position as decreed by the two women. The fact that the patient can no longer reach any of these items fails to register with the women, it does not matter as long as everything is in its place and in their opinion there is a place for everything. When the bed space is at last in perfect order the two women turn their attentions to the now worried patient. In a blur of movement, combs, shaving razors and tooth brushes appear as the patient is groomed like a second hand car on a dealers plot. At last both patient and bed space meet the approval of the two women and the patient is allowed to rest as they retake their seats, and promptly begin talking across him. The husband and father lies quietly on the bed, hoping and praying that no other small item of his attire, his bed, his cupboard or his food and drink supplies catch their attention again. In fact the worn out patient barely mutters a word to either of the two women in fear of what it may initiate. He lays quietly, sometimes pretending to be asleep as he wishes and waits for the visiting period to be over, an end to his torment.

Male visitors to a female ward present another story. The man enters the ward and glances about the room in case a younger and prettier patient catches his eye. Not that he would dare be caught showing an interest in another, but the interest is there all the same, hidden hopefully from his present spouse, partner, girlfriend or mistress. After an initial kiss of greeting, the male normally does not initiate any further contact, responding only when his hand is grasped and held vice like by the woman lying despondently in the hospital bed. There is no straightening of bed covers or changing of night clothes. Food and drink may be inspected in case of replenishment or as refreshment for the starving husband or partner who has been unsuccessfully fending for himself while at home alone. If a command to remove soiled clothing, unconsumed food or discarded books and magazines arises, the male smiles obligingly but his face portrays his discomfort as each item is placed into a plastic carrier bag for the trip home.

The male visitor will often bring in that days newspapers, which he then reads himself, he may bring in fresh food supplies, which he then helps himself to, or he may stare vacantly into space, wishing away the visiting hours while attempting to continue a contrived conversation with his loved one. His care and love are evident but his discomfort, fear and concern presented by the poor health of his spouse or partner, the unfamiliar surroundings of the hospital and the utter feeling of helplessness at the situation conflict with his male emotions, bringing confusion and sorrow.

As a patient lying surrounded by tedium and the monotonous existence of the hospital ward, watching the staff, fellow patients and their visitors quickly becomes a major form of interest. From the position of my bed I could clearly see the main doors into the ward and this fact proved to be of great interest to someone sadly lacking in mental simulation as myself. Watching visitors pour into the ward, assumptions and judgements of each one sprung uncharitably to mind.

First to catch my observations are those visitors who refused to follow signs or simply ask for directions. Tribes of noisy families, confused spouses, secret girl/boyfriends or work mates flock onto the ward hoping that their own sense of direction will lead them to their intended destination. An impossible task as they have never entered this part of the hospital before in their lives! But it was an elderly couple who caught my eye as they came through the doors and stood still, hardly moving a muscle, they just stood. Anxiously their eyes searched the immediate environment, faces throwing lost and uncertain glances at everyone who passed by them. Two little old people stood just inside the doors on a busy and bustling modern ward. Patients, other visitors and staff passed them by without a thought, until finally one nurse was struck by their immobility. Quietly she approached them and sought their desired destination. Suddenly she recoiled in shock!

'You want to go where?' she almost shouted.

'The fertility clinic,' was the soft reply from the elderly gentleman.

Ok, all those without visitors heard this so our ears perked up and our interested knew no bounds. The picture of a quite elderly couple, standing forlornly by the doors and requesting directions to the fertility clinic was something straight out of a TV comedy show. And it was happening right in front of us.

'I'm sorry,' said the nurse in the now very silent ward, 'Did you say the fertility clinic?'

'Yes please, can you direct us?'

'But we don't have a fertility clinic, it's in the private hospital, not here,' stated the still shocked nurse.

'Oh dear, we naturally assumed it would be in this hospital. Now we're going to be late,' the elderly lady responded with a glance at her husband.

'Never mind dear, we'll ring them from the lobby and let them know we're coming. Thank you for your help nurse, but we must be on our way now.'

'Hang on a moment please?' asked the nurse, 'Are you sure you want that particular clinic?

'Yes that's the one. We have spent much of the day travelling and we would like to get to the clinic as soon as possible. So thank you again but we must go,' replied the old man.

The attention of the ward was now so fixed on this conversation patients and visitors alike, and the unthinkable images it portrayed in everyone's mind caused nurses to stop mid duty, patients to leave urine bottles dangling and food and drink to dribble down chins from open mouths. I nearly fell out of bed as I craned forward as much as possible to ensure I did not miss one morsel of conversation during the exchange. Even the senior doctors and a consultant ceased their interpretations of medical conditions and treatment to listen to what we all considered was a clear impossibility.

'Excuse me,' pleaded the nurse, 'I must ask; why do you want the fertility clinic?'

The elderly couple glanced at each other, they obviously realised the consternation their request had caused. They smiled at each other and grasped each others hand. With a twinkle in his eye and a slight smile on his old face, the old man turned to look about himself before looking back at the perplexed nurse.

'We've come to meet our daughter at the clinic, she works there. Why? Whatever did you think we wanted with the place?'

With a giggle the elderly couple pushed open the doors and left our ward. Up roar ensued within the ward!

As mentioned before, visitors to hospitals come in all shapes and sizes, fat, thin, short and tall, young or old, male or female or those that cannot decide. Few cause eye brows to rise amongst staff or fellow patients', it is mainly the actions and activities of some visitors that provide bored patients with some light entertainment. There are often surprises as the constant flow of people going into or going out of a major hospital number in many thousands each and every day. A good number of these transient persons work at the hospital and care for others in their own specific way, including nurses, doctors, porters carrying, cleaners cleaning, office workers creating paper mountains and caterers ruining food. For every patient there is a huge diversity of people with jobs that assist in the care of that patient, even clerical managers have been known to help in some small way, though this is seldom seen. All peoples from all races, creeds and career choice create a living, vibrant environment within the hospital, and the daily visitors are all just part of the strange mix amongst the human throng.

Those who work in hospitals have seen just about everything, every situation and every variety of people in the process of their working day. Unlike the poor patient who's knowledge or experience lacks the familiarity gained by the hospitals work force. Such an example happened in our ward with the overnight admission of a new patient. As he was admitted during the early hours of the morning, many of us did not even know he was there until we were awoken at the ungodly hour of six o'clock in the morning.

The night nurses begin their morning duties quite early in the morning to ensure all chores and tasks are completed before their shift ends and the day staff begin. Our initial awakening comes when a nurse rushes hurriedly into our ward to collect and empty any urine bottles used during the night. Toiletry chores completed the nurse grabs a mobile monitoring machine and moving from patient to patient begins to record our general state of health via pulse, blood pressure, saturated oxygen levels and temperature. This done we all nod off again until re-awoken by the rattle of the medicine trolley pushed by a tired staff nurse into the ward. The first pills, potions and brews of the day are then quickly administered before the nurse rushes out and into the next ward.

We nod off once more just as the cleaner marches cheerfully into the ward with her cleaning trolley and begins mopping floors, wiping surfaces and greeting each bleary eyed patient with loud morning salutations. The cleaner moves around each bed with practiced skill, though with little concern about the noise she creates while bashing mops against beds, running taps while cleaning sinks and all with a brightness that should be banned at that hour of the morning. Her chores completed she leaves the room and we all attempt to recapture sleep yet again. Only to be re-woken as both the night staff and the day staff wander in and proceed to do their reports. This is done whenever there is a staff or shift change. The soon to be off duty night staff give a report on each patient to the day staff, how the patient has slept over night, what medication they are on and any vital information regarding the patient's condition. After reporting on every patient, the nurses leave us in peace and once again we attempt to sleep, just as the breakfast trolley barges in! The time is now only seven thirty and we are already shattered from the original awakening at six o'clock and the constant interruptions since then.

It was only then, while we munched on the first meal of the day, that we began to pay any real attention to our new fellow patient. The first things we noticed was the deep tan covering his entire body, or at least what we could see, was a rich golden brown, burnt by long hours in the sun. The other two features to stand out were his pure white, collar length hair and the jingling items of gold jewellery that hung from his neck and both wrists. The trappings of a young man maybe, but our new ward buddy appeared to be well into his late sixties or early seventies, a fact borne out but the wide girth of his midriff.

Breakfast over we began to chat, enquiring his name and where did he lived. He appeared quite a pleasant guy and happily informed us how he had ended up in hospital and offered many details about himself, in fact he did not seem to be in any hurry to stop talking! He told us of his recent travels to exotic countries, his lavish holidays and how he really did not want to be in hospital again as he had only been discharged two days before. We of course took all travel stories with just a little cynicism, he was obviously quite ill and no longer a young man, nor in fact even a middle aged man. We happily joined in with the charade though, after all, entertainment is scarce in a hospital ward. Banter relating to his sun tan and the length of his hair continued sporadically throughout the morning, including some less than discreet remakes about his profusion of gold arranged like Christmas tree decorations about his person. The new patient, who stated his name was Jimmy, took all the verbal exchanges in good humour and returned as good as he got, hence our liking and respect for him was quickly sealed. Despite all the jokes, innuendos and speculation, Jimmy had one more surprise for us, and visiting time was to be the hour for his grand acclaim.

During the morning nurses ensured everyone had some form of wash or shower, dragging we patients from our beds and frog marching us to the shower room, or providing wash bowls and materials for anyone who was not well enough to walk yet. When the nurses approached Jimmy and inquired if he was to sort himself out with a wash or shower, or did he need assistance, he shook his head and informed them that his wife would be in later and she was bring all his washing materials and that she would help him as well. Jimmy was quite ill; it was obvious as he could not even comb his long white hair without difficulty. Having a relative attend to a patients hygiene care is not unusual so the nurses were happy to leave him to the care of his wife and let him rest.

The majority of the other patients were capable of self ablutions so the line for the shower room grew. While we were otherwise engaged the nurses quickly made our beds and tidied our bed space before we returned and messed everything up again. Doctors did their rounds; lunch and medication were delivered with little disruption, followed by our enforced hours rest before the visitors descended upon us. Virtually all of us were expecting visitors of some description, wives, mistresses, children, friends and the odd religious visitor who prayed on those alone.

At two o'clock the ward doors burst open and in strode the first of the visitors and it was not long before the ward was filled with the sound of muted inane chatter. Luckily the week day afternoon visiting period only appeared to attract immediate relatives and spouses, it was weekends and evenings that hoards of kids, strange relatives and people off the street wandered in, adding to the noise and confusion of the ward. Jimmy's visitor had not yet arrived but he appeared unconcerned, he had borrowed a newspaper from the chap in the next bed and was busy trying to separate the truth from the sensationalism contained within the tabloid.

Fifteen minutes after the start of visiting hours, the doors opened and all the males in the ward gaped in amazement. Through the doors floated a vision, an absolute beauty walked in and paused as she glanced round to establish her bearings. The new visitor was probably in her very early thirties, tall, slim and very shapely. Blond hair encircled a perfectly made up face and all her assets were emphasized and in the correct proportions. Her tight fitting white blouse tucked securely into a short kilt like skirt and calf high boots reached just below the knees on long legs, a long necklace hung suggestively between her breasts and a red designer hand bag was slung over one shoulder. The only item that appeared slightly out of place in this perfect vision was a plastic carrier bag held in one hand.

A stunned silence collapsed over the ward, every male, both patient and visitor alike stared in admiration as the blond bombshell entered our ward, wives, girlfriends and daughters glaring at husbands and sons as they realised the cause of this sudden cessation of all talk and attention. Bulges began to appear under bed sheets and those men sitting on chairs or stood beside beds quickly shifted position in an attempt to hide their natural male reaction to the sight that had enraptured their eyes. The cause of this activity wiggled into the ward and headed for Jimmy who had looked up from his paper with a smile. The beautiful woman leaned over and planted a kiss on Jimmy's lips that oozed sexual promise.

'Hello dear,' he greeted.

'Hi Jimmy,' she replied as she picked a chair from the stack by the ward door and carried it over to his bedside.

'How are you today? Is there any improvement yet?'

'Yep, the doc's say I should be home soon. How are the kids? Who's looking after them while you're here?'

'Ho they're fine, your mother is looking after them and I think she's taking them to the park. Everyone sends their love and wishes; the kids are missing you and want you home soon.'

'That's nice,' said Jimmy with a smile, 'What about you? How are you, are you coping?'

'Of course I am no worries. You just hurry up and get better so you can come home.'

'Yes dear,' replied Jimmy.

The conversation continued between them as our attention was brought sharply back to our own individual visitors. Our attention regained via elbows being dug into ribs, slaps on fidgeting hands and pinches on arms by spouses and other loved ones who had grown tired of being ignored in favour of the stunning woman by Jimmy's bed. Things got worse and our imaginations went wild as the lovely young lady drew clean pyjamas, washing equipment, slippers and a towel from the carrier bag. Still chatting she then drew the curtains around Jimmy's bed and from their conversation we knew she was helping the lucky guy to wash and change. The discreet section of the ablutions completed, she opened to curtains again before climbing onto Jimmy's bed, short skirt revealing firm flesh as she positioned herself in a kneeing stance behind Jimmy on the bed. With great care and affection she retrieved a brush from the bag and began gently brushing his long white hair. Seeing this delicious woman knelt on the bed with a total disregard for how this scene was affecting the other male patients and visitors caused temperatures and blood pressures to rise alarmingly! And not only amongst the male occupants of the ward, though the rising blood pressure in the female relatives mirrored their rising tempers as they watched their men salivate or just plainly drool.

Visiting time progressed and each of the patients tried desperately to pay full attention to the person who had chosen to visit them on that day, while surreptitiously casting longing glances at Jimmy and the woman. One and three quarter hours later the visiting period came to a close, all wives, husbands, girlfriends, friends and assorted relatives began their journey home. Once the ward was clear Jimmy was bombarded with questions.

'Hey Jimmy! Who was that girl? Your daughter?' queried one of the patients.

'No,' replied Jimmy as he began settling down in his bed to rest. 'That's the wife. We've been married for about 10 years and we have two kids, one seven and the other is nine, both boys.'

'So you married when she was about twenty?' asked the guy in the bed next to Jimmy.

'Yeah, in fact she was just twenty when we married. I was looking for someone younger but beggars can't be choosers,' he replied with a sigh.

'What?' I exclaimed, 'Too old at twenty! What age girl did you want then?'

'Oh; sixteen to eighteen would have been nice, but I suppose twenty isn't too far off. Anyway she's a nice girl and looks after me well enough, so I can't complain.'

'Too old at only twenty!' Steve almost shouted, 'What the hell are you talking about? I would love a twenty year old snuggling up to me. And you're complaining she was too old!'

'I'm joking,' replied Jimmy with a grin.

'OK,' said Steve from the corner bed, 'I gotta know, how old are you Jimmy? If you don't mind me asking? Bugger it, I don't care if you mind, I've really gotta know!'

'That's alright, I'm sixty five, sixty six in two months time actually.'

A stunned silence blanketed the ward for several minutes. Jimmy continued getting comfortable in his bed, failing to notice the pure shock, and much envy, that displayed on every other face in the ward.

'Ah. You must be quite wealthy then?' questioned Steve bluntly.

'Not as such; no,' replied Jimmy with just a hint of annoyance becoming visible on his face.

'Aw come on. How the hell did you get such an attractive and young wife at your age if you're not rich?' continued Steve.

Obviously rattled now by questions he must have answered dozens of times by jealous men, Jimmy sat up in his bed and glared at each of us, daring us to pry any further into his private life.

'Look! We met while I was on holiday in Greece. She was the tour guide and we hit it off immediately! There are no hidden motives between us, I am not rich and she is not a gold digger! We have been married ten years and we're still happy! Got it? That's enough; keep your noses out of my business please!'

With that angry retort, Jimmy slumped down into his bed and pulled up the covers, making it quite plain he was going to say no more about his stunning young wife.

Silence reigned over our ward as each of the other patients devoured this information. Personally I was pleased. Pleased that an older man could find love with a much younger woman without any strings attached. I could see some of the others were not so believing, disbelief, envy and even anger was evident, but some also shared my opinion. Good luck to the guy and his wife, he was a likable chap and I saw no reason why the fact he had won a wife so young and so beautiful should cause resentment or anger. Envy yes! Some jealously yes! After all I am a red blooded male as well, but anger or resentment no. Besides, the image of that beautiful woman pleasured my most fanciful dreams for a long time. Imagination is a wonderful thing.

Things soon returned to normality in the ward, Jimmy regained his cheerfulness and chatter, providing no one broached the subject of his wife. Tedium became the order of the day once more, but now there were additional breaks in the monotony of a hospital ward, visiting time. Excluding Jimmy, all the other patients eagerly waited each visiting period, and for a short time, until Jimmy was finally discharged, even the number of male visitors attending our ward reached record levels.

Visitors are an important factor in the well being and recovery of patients, loved ones, friends, family or even the friends made of fellow patients visitors contribute to the overall benefit of those suffering. Although most visitors to hospitals do so out of love, or friendship or respect, hospitals would be much poorer places of recovery if not for them. So if you are unlucky enough to be entrapped in a modern motel of marvellous medicine, be nice to your visitors, be polite to the screaming families and try not to condemn the antics of others, no matter how loud, irritating or uncaring they appear. Give your full attention to those who have made the effort to visit you in your hour of need and try not to stare and dribble in envy, lust or complete fascination at another patient's spouse!

Chapter Nine: Forbidden Passion

Although it can often appear otherwise, not all male patients are middle
to old age, young men also require the delights of hospital admission
occasionally. Having a young man in his twenties on their ward always
seems to brighten the nurses' day and send us older patients into despair
as we remember our own youth. Certainly the sight of attractive nurses,
some younger doctors, blue rinse cleaners and the odd, very odd male
hospital porter fawning over the strapping young man brings on the
incurable disease of envy!

Lying peacefully on his bed, the use of a pyjama jacket
scorned, preferring instead to demonstrate his bronzed pectoral muscles
and tight *six pack* to the world at large, the young man was obviously
enjoying the attention. When stood he reached just less than six foot
tall, slim waisted, dark hair and chocolate brown eyes smiled out over
perfectly white teeth. To add injury to insult, the male model look-a-
like was pleasant, intelligent and charming. We more mature, saggy
and wrinkled patients hated him immediately. In fairness this was not
true, we all found the young man to be extremely nice, willing to help
us older folk where possible and appeared genuinely friendly.

The young Adonis was called Carl and worked in the business
of finance, though he never once elaborated on exactly what he did in
finance, and we did not enquire too deeply in case he decided to tell us.
Finance to most is a particularly boring subject. He did inform us of
where he lived and that he had a girlfriend and they were trying for a
baby. They already had a house and mortgage and starting a family was
next on the list.

The young couple was attempting to use the Rhythm Method,
or Standard day's method to give it another name, to improve the

chances of conception. These methods encourage sexual activity during the woman's highest fertility period thus ensuring intercourse is most productive. So for a set time each month when it is judged that his girlfriend was particularly fertile, they went at it like rabbits!

Feelings of envy aside, I realised I had no idea why he was in hospital, maybe his girlfriend had worn him out? I wondered, though seeing his superb physical condition I did not consider this assumption for too long.

'So why are you in here then Carl?' I asked politely.

'Some type of tests I think,' Carl replied, 'they think I may have a blood disorder, least that's what the doc called it. Dunno what it is though.'

'So how long do they intend keeping you in hospital for?' I enquired.

'About a bloody week!' he retorted with a hint of annoyance, 'It's the time of the month when me and my girlfriend are supposed to be trying to get her pregnant. Bit difficult with me stuck in here.'

'Yeah, I can see it may cause the odd inconvenience,' I sympathised somewhat smugly.

Although Carl had been admitted two days ago, we had seen no sign of his girlfriend, Carl had initially stated she did not like hospitals and would not be visiting him. Several of us wrinkly patients were disappointed at this; we concluded she must be a stunner. Someone with Carl's handsome looks and perfect physic would surely attract another of equal physical perfection. Out of earshot from Carl, our imaginations ran wild with speculation on her looks, her figure and her chosen attire. We imagined long flowing blond hair, an hour glass figure and scantily dressed in a tight fitting blouse over a short skirt and long legs. Roughly the normal way men see girls in their fantasies, well maybe just me, but I doubt it.

Breakfast had just concluded and we were all attempting to snatch a last moment or two in bed before the morning nurses invaded our sanctuary and sternly marched us out to the bathroom for our daily hose down. Most of the patients on the ward were mobile and thus required to perform their ablutions personally, only two patients could not and so a nurse would bring in a bowl, water and cleaning equipment so they could wash in bed. Sadly the days of bed baths by teams of lovely nurses are long gone. One can still get a bed bath but only if one is too ill to notice or even care.

Carl was one of the patients not allowed go to the bathroom unassisted. Although he appeared truly physically fit, the doctors were concerned enough about his as yet undiagnosed condition that he had been recently confined to bed and only allowed a trip to the bathroom or toilet via wheel chair with an attending nurse, much to Carl's embarrassment.

This morning Carl stated that he did not really feel up to washing and that he would get someone to help him shower after lunch. The period following breakfast in hospitals can be a very busy time. Getting patients out of bed, dressed if possible, making and or changing beds, changing various dressings and bandages, sorting out arrangements for any patients being discharged, moved to another ward, or requiring x-rays, CT scans or autopsies takes a terrific toll on the staff. Doctors strutting in and out of the ward as they examined the progress of their patients, cleaners attempting to complete their chores amidst the chaos, the paper man doing his rounds selling newspapers, sweets and drinks, and the dreaded phlebotomists attacking all on their lists. So when Carl offered to wait till afternoon for his obligatory wash, the nurses did not complain, but hide their disappointment at the lost opportunity to admire such a perfect body.

During the morning I noticed no signs that Carl was unwell, he appeared to me to be as fit as he seemed yesterday, but I am not a doctor so what do I know. Lunch time came and went and a staff change occurred for those nurses working a split shift. Those who began work at the crack of dawn were readying to sign off; the replacements arriving would work late into the evening. An uneventful staffing exchange occurred that went un-noticed by the patients, including me. The first I knew was a pretty young nurse just returned from her days off entered the ward, and I know she had not been there in the morning. Her greeting to us all confirmed that she had just started and was on the late shift.

Emily was not a qualified nurse, she was a Health Care Assistant, or HCA and it was obvious that this day she was designated to work mainly in our bay of the ward. Emily was in her early twenties with long nut brown hair and huge almond eyes. A pretty face topped a shapely figure, least we assumed she was shapely because her uniform hide more than we liked! Emily was a very pleasant girl whom any man would wish for his daughter, girlfriend or mistress.

Emily had barely finished greeting all the patients when Carl called her to him and requested help in his ablutions. With a smile Emily disappeared from the ward in search of a wheelchair, reappearing almost immediately and stood ready as Carl climbed into the contraption. Grasping towels, wash bag and new pyjama trousers, Emily pushed Carl out to the man's washroom in the ward corridor. No one commented on the silence that flowed the pair from our room, but we all knew we were seething was jealousy inside, all wishing we were that young man.

It was about thirty minutes later that I realised the two young people had not yet returned. How long does it take a young strong man to have a shower I wondered, but these days who knows? Many men spend as much time preening themselves than women are reputed to do, sometimes even longer. But just then the pair emerged from the washroom and Emily quietly wheeled Carl back to his bed. With a gentle touch and a caring soul she straightened his bedclothes and sought assurance that he was comfortable and had all he needed, to which he replied he did and gave his thanks. Emily then departed the room in search of other chores to complete.

Returned to the peace of the ward and the comfort of his bed, Carl quickly went off to sleep. We all assumed the rigors of the washroom have exhausted him and ensured we did nothing to disturb him. An hour later he was awake and back to his normal self, chatting and joking with us in a pleasant manner.

Emily constantly came into our bay, checking on us patients and undertaking such chores as fetching urine bottles, commodes, straightening beds and restraining those patients attempting to make a stealthy escape. It was obvious to all that Emily took her duties seriously; none could say she ignored our pleas or nursing care, but I did notice Carl received the biggest smiles and in truth I could not blame her, a young man amidst we wrinklies.

The next day Emily was on the early shift and straight after breakfast Carl requested help to get to the washroom and have his shower. Again it was Emily that volunteered to perform the task, and once again I noticed the length of time it took them to re-emerge onto our bay. The following day it was the same, Emily taking Carl for his shower.

By now some of the other patients had noticed both the regularity and the length of time taken by Emily and Carl, so it was not long before the jokes began to surface. Carl calmly took the jibes in good humour, playing along with us but insisting nothing untoward was happening and that Emily was simply a nice person doing her job. Emily herself also laughed off the odd comment from us older, less attractive and crinkled patients, stating that if any of us needed help in washing, she would give us the same amount of care. Of course every one of us requested her aid in our bodily cleansing routines immediately. Alas to no avail, she politely but firmly declined adding that doctors orders were required before a nurse could accompany a patient into the washroom.

The following day Emily was off duty and it was noted that Carl elected to have a simple bed wash this time, he had showered three days in a row and considered that enough, and he would possibly shower the next day.

'I supposed you've gotten used to a helping hand?' I asked him with a smile.

'Well I admit the help is nice,' he replied, 'especially when assisted by some one so attractive. I do still find it embarrassing and strange having someone standing outside the shower cubicle while I wash and someone in the room with me as I get dressed.'

'Ahh they've seen it all before mate,' laughed another patient, 'Bet you haven't got anything we haven't.'

'I bet he has! Age hasn't shrivelled him yet I'm sure,' I rejoined with a laugh as Carl flushed a pale shade of red.

'I wouldn't mind a pretty young nurse giving me a sponge bath, I might even rise to the occasion for the first time in years!' added another patient with a wistful grin.

'Come on you dirty lot, give the boy a break. It's not his fault all the young nurses are swooning over him, and I think I would find it embarrassing having someone watch me shower. Even the wife! But knowing her, she would just nag that I'd missed a bit.' I said.

'Yep Mine too!' agreed several around the room.

'Huh! Mine would probably come armed with a wire brush and a magnifying glass, just to be sure,' groaned the patient next to me.

Carl listened and smiled at each comment, he even laughed at one or two, but he was obviously uncomfortable with our jokes so with a final grin, we changed the subject and left him in peace.

At last came the day when the doctors decided the tests were clear and Carl could be discharged. It was concluded that he had a virus, not a blood infection so he was to be sent home with instructions to see his local doctor at the earliest opportunity. Carl of course was delighted and his grin spread from ear to ear as he readied himself for home. Emily was off duty again this day so many of us remarked on how disappointed she would be when she came back and found him gone.

Carl did not care, with a knowing smile he informed us his girlfriend was finally coming to the hospital to pick him up so we would all get to meet her. Just as he had finished packing his bags, Emily walked into our ward. She was dressed in simple jeans and T-shirt with her coat folded over her arm. Surprised looks from both staff and patients were ignored as she threw her arms around Carl's neck and planted a huge kiss on his cheek.

'Have you met my girlfriend?' asked Carl with a grin.

'Well you bugger!' came the politest of exclamations at this news.

'Yep, we decided not to tell anyone about our relationship otherwise I would have been sent to another ward. The management don't like their staff treating relatives, in case of misadventure or favouritism,' smiled Carl as he hugged Emily tight.

'OK, fair enough,' I said with the acknowledging nods from my fellow patients.

'I suppose you'll be able to get on with starting a family now?' asked the patient in the bed next to mine.

'Definitely the first thing on our list,' smiled Carl as Emily blushed and looked down at the floor in embarrassment.

At this point realisation hit me, 'But you've carried on trying for a family while you've been in here, haven't you Carl?' I asked with a knowing grin.

'Dunno what you mean mate. Anyway we're off so all the best to each of you and I hope you all recover soon.'

This said, Carl and Emily left our bay, rapidly heading out the doors into the corridor before any of the surprised staff could comment on their behaviour. A light giggle from Emily could be heard wafting in from the corridor as the two disappeared. In a stunned silence both patients and staff tried to grasp what had just happened.

'Well what'd you make of that?' exclaimed a gray haired patient in the bed near the door.

'Wonder if Emily was his girlfriend all alone, or if he didn't really have one before. Maybe that's why his *girlfriend* never visited him?' pondered the chap next to Carl's vacant bed.

'Huh! With his looks maybe he's hoping to juggle both!' replied the gray haired patient.

'Well that's a new name for it. Juggling! I can think of much more descriptive terms for having two girlfriends,' enjoined another patient with a lopsided grin.

'Whatever, I think they are suited for one another. Both of them are young, fit and good looking. Makes you sick dunnit!' concluded Carl's ex bed neighbour.

During this exchange I had remained quiet, not wishing to put my thoughts into words, and it would not be decent to allow my realisation to become the subject of coarse or ribald comments and speculation. Nor did I wish any consequences to befall Emily when she returned to work, if I voiced my conclusions, her employment may be in peril, so I held my own council and remained quiet while the speculation and jokes continued amongst the patients, and most likely the staff also.

I had realised what had been happening under our very own noses, the reason why Carl waited for Emily before accepting assistance in his daily ablutions. I understood why neither Carl nor Emily wanted to make their relationship known to staff or patients. I wished them both success in their efforts to start a family, both would make great parents. I also know why Carl and Emily took so long in the washroom, but I am not saying.

Chapter Ten: One man Brass band.

On a recent visit to a scene of confusion and bewilderment, commonly
known as a medical admissions ward, I encountered a night like never
before. All around me the usual noises of a busy hospital screamed
through the hours of darkness. Most of these sounds were very familiar
to me and my tired brain automatically screened out the distractions.

On this night there was an exception, in the bed next to mine
lay a mature gentleman of whom I can offer no description. The curtain
screen between us remained in position for my entire short stay, the
gentleman obviously not of a social nature. This is not unusual when a
patient is first admitted as doctors often come and go frequently as they
consider their assessment of the patient, before asking another doctor
what they should do. A patient's relatives habitually hang around
during these first few hours, especially those unfamiliar with the long,
long process of admission and diagnosis, made much longer during the
night time hours. The chap adjacent to me had no visitors, and I
concluded he had been brought in just before my arrival. What ever his
reason for being in hospital were not obviously apparent, nothing
unusual in this as not all patients admitted into hospital scream, moan or
bleed everywhere. My only wish was that he did not snore at 100
decibels, fart like a horse or wander aimless around the ward all night.
As far as I was concerned he was simply another patient awaiting the
medical delights of the over worked junior night doctor. He had my
sympathy as I too awaited the attentions of a tired, confused and over
whelmed young medical school graduate. I settled down to sleep in
anticipation of a long night ahead of me.

Barely was I unconscious for a minute before being woken as
my attention was grabbed suddenly to the gentleman next to me. He
was singing! The night was dark, the staff were busy, the other

patients' were suffering or trying to sleep and the patient next to me was singing! Not words, lyrics or any recognisable song, the gentleman was pouring out at full volume what could only be described as an imitation of a brass band. Har-pa-rum, papa, Par-rum rappata! Not only one brass instrument, oh no, this guy had assignations to be an entire brass band all on his own!

With the sound of trumpets, cornets, tuba, euphonium and trombone already echoing through the silence, a drum section enjoined with gusto. Tap, tap, tap, soon became slap then thump, thump, thump as the gentleman increased his rhythm accompaniment to a crescendo. Striking any inanimate object within reach, he hammered out a beat to accompany the blaring brass ensemble. The fact that sick or injured people were desperately trying to seek refuge and relief in sleep, ignoring the obvious fact that he was in a hospital ward, or the fact that it was well into the late night hours when he began his band parade appeared not to bother the pa-rum papa man. On he played throughout the night in full volume, despite the objections from myself and the only other conscious patient in the bay. Snatches of a tune could occasionally be identified but on the whole it was purely random bursts of par-rum papa-rum accompanied by the slap or thump of inert objects that served as percussion.

The only interruption to the estranged singing came when the gentleman decided to remind all within a hundred metre radius that he was actually supposed to be in pain. Trumpets were exchanged for groans, trombones replaced with moans and the drum beat ceased in favour of curses. Calls for a nurse to request more pain killers thundered through the ward until the appropriate medication was administered and the one man brass band once more entered at stage right. On and on until morning the brass section continued, coming to a final cessation when breakfast arrived. But the final curtain call came when the lady driving the breakfast trolley politely enquired if the gentleman had sleep well.

'Didn't sleep a wink all night!' he groaned, 'Too damn noisy in this place!'

Chapter Eleven: Strange events . . . . *One.*

Alice is a friend who I have known for some years now. She also makes frequent visits to hospital as an inpatient and told me these two stories during one of our chats. As a background to her stories, Alice explained that she had been admitted into hospital recently once again and after a few days of treatment was now on the road to recovery. As with all hospitals up and down the country, life can be very boring in the stage between recovery and discharge. Alice was in a stage of pure tedium so any conversation, behaviour or event out of the ordinary was highly prized, and this day was to be Alice's lucky day.

Now rumours abound that women like to chat, talk and gossip. I cannot possibly comment on this as I am married to one and my life may be at risk if I do. Let's just say that women initiate a conversation with a stranger faster than most males would. So when a new patient arrived in Alice's ward, it was not long before the patient who gave her name as Betty, was in full conversation with all the other inhabitants of the ward. Within moments everyone knew Betty's name, age, where she lived and that she was married. Details from each of the patients soon followed as all those who had not previously shared their life story did so now, before anyone had the opportunity to fall blissfully asleep.

The ward was not yet full to capacity so the chat between the ladies could be labelled as an intimate tête-à-tête rather than a full blown natter. Empty hospital beds do not remain so for long and Betty was the first new comer of the day, but another was certain to arrive shortly. It has been known on odd occasion for an in coming patient to be sat tolerantly beside a bed waiting for the present occupier to leave. There are seldom any beds vacant for long in today's NHS, though the Fracture ward tended to have less of a waiting list than some other wards, even so any empty bed is expected to be filled almost immediately.

By now the ladies were in full vocal swing and so it was not long before someone enquired how Betty had ended up there. Taking a deep breath, Betty plunged into her monologue.

'Well I was just coming out of church actually,' she began, 'It had been such a nice meeting as well, shame how it ended though.'

'Why? How did it end?' asked a patient.

'I was on my way home, I only live a couple of streets away and as it was a warm sunny evening, I felt quite happy to walk. My husband normally picks me up if it's wet or dark. He says he doesn't want me walking home on dark nights in case I frighten any poor muggers that may be innocently lurking with intent. He's a cheeky begger,' laughed Betty.

'Cheeky! I'd thump him if he were mine,' commented Alice.

'Me too!' responded one of the other patients.

'No, he's a dear really. He loves to make me laugh and always comes out with little quips like that. Once we thought we had a burglar in our house, my husband sent me to investigate downstairs; he said I would scare away any robbers faster than he could. He's a real joker, really.'

'Huh! I'll bet,' Alice whispered to the patient next to her, 'I'd kill him!' replied the neighbour.

'Anyway,' interrupted Betty sharply, 'as I said, it was a lovely meeting. We prayed for the healing of one member who was taken ill and rushed to hospital. We all spoke about our experiences, and then we had refreshments. It wasn't a proper church meeting, more of a social get together and I certainly enjoyed it.'

Betty paused to ease herself into a more comfortable position in her bed before continuing.

'I left the meeting about nine thirty and started walking home. I suppose I wasn't paying any attention on where I was walking because before I knew it, I had tripped on a manhole thing and broken my leg! Someone had taken the cover off and not replaced it correctly. I felt such a fool.'

'Maybe kids had been playing with it?' Alice wondered.

'No, I did see some workmen there on my way to church. I think they were checking a water pipe or something. It was most likely one of them that didn't replace the cover properly.'

'Plonkers!' said Alice to the accompaniment of other such derogatory comments from round the room.

'Next thing I know I was in the Emergency department getting my leg plastered,' continued Betty.

'So how come you're in this ward? They don't normally keep you in just for a broken leg,' asked Alice in puzzlement.

'They think I might have twisted my knee as well but they can't tell at the moment so they're keeping me in so it can be checked properly in a day or so.'

'OK. As a matter of interest and you don't need to tell me if you don't want to, what church was it? Catholic, Methodist or Synagogue?'

'Spiritualist actually,' was the unexpected replied.

'Well bugger me!' exclaimed Alice.

Silence followed Alice's outburst as each on the ward attempted to formalise the questions that were whirling in their minds. Everyone knew and understood the usual bag of church nominations, such as the Catholics, the Church of England, Islam and Methodists and even Scientology, but Spiritualist was new to many of us. Of course we had all heard of spiritualism but a church based on spiritualism was unknown to us at that time. The immediate vision plaguing our imagination was of an old woman dressed in a shawl, large ear rings and colourful head scarf peering into a crystal ball. Our minds played pictures showing dozens of such women, each sitting at a little table with their shiny crystal ball before them, all lined up like pews in a Christian church.

'Okay. Not heard of that before. So what sort of thing do you get up to in your Spiritualist church then?' asked Alice when curiosity finally overcame her.

'Oh, it's not what you think I'll bet,' replied Betty, 'We pray for the healing of those sick or hurt, we try to help build bridges between those living and loved ones that have passed on, we meditate and practice clairvoyance. It's all very interesting and does no one any harm. In fact the Spiritualist Church has been involved in many events over the last hundred or so years. We were active in the temperance and anti-capital punishment lobbies, in the advocacy of women's rights and female suffrage and we have churches all over the world.'

'Ahh! How come you didn't see your little trip coming then?'

'We're not fortune tellers!' snapped Betty, 'We simply believe in spiritual communication and try to use what ever knowledge we gain for the good of all.'

'Sorry, didn't mean to offend, I just couldn't resist the old cliché,' smiled Alice in apology.

'That's OK,' said Betty, 'Funny though, the man in charge of our church did foresee I would meet someone with the same problem as me very soon. I wonder if he meant you lot.'

'Doubt it,' replied Alice, 'Falling on an inspection cover doesn't seem the sort of important information one would expect to receive from the spirit world. At least not in my opinion.'

'I expect you're right. Just bad luck I decided to walk home instead of dragging my husband away from his telly. Next time he can damn well come and get me!' Betty ended forcefully.

'Good for you girl,' Alice replied to the agreement of the other patients in the ward.

The conversation soon switched to other much more important items of concern, like what happened on Coronation Street the night before and who was the next character to be killed off in Eastenders. The topic of husbands and partners followed as each woman commented favourably or the reverse on their respective spouse's employment and capabilities around the home and in the bed room. Most were considered to have failed miserably. It did cause somewhat of a stir when Betty announced her husband was a scientist. Not the normal mix found in marriages, science and spiritualism, but Betty could see no problems with their different paths of religion and logic. Alice decided Betty was either a kindly soul who saw the world through rose tinted glasses, or was really obtuse and did not have a clue about the possible conflict of interests. When Alice commented on this difference of interests, Betty stated that her husband was happy with the situation as it initiated conversations around a variety of subjects diverse to both of them. Alice had to admit defeat.

Nurses suddenly appeared in the ward causing the conversation to die down, each patient too interested on what was to happen next. The two nurses began readying the remaining empty bed, obviously for a new incoming patient. Alice, Betty and the other ward residents waited eagerly. The possibility of more gossip and chat looming on the horizon being almost overcome by the ghoulish fascination at the prospect of a serious illness or injury that they could verbally dissect. Almost before the two nurses had completed their task, the new patient was wheeled in and helped gently onto the bed. From the plaster cast on her right leg, it was clear what had happened to her, but as yet no one knew the details. It would not be long. Once the nurse's had left after settling her in, the questions began to flow. Her name came first, which was Joyce, then came the questions as to why she had been admitted.

'I've broken my leg,' announced Joyce even though it was quite plain to see, 'and they think I have damaged my pelvis so I have to have an x-ray and stay in for a day or so.'

'How did you manage that?' asked Alice, who was the most curious of the ward, 'Or were you doing something you shouldn't? Not jumping off wardrobes I hope?' she laughed.

'No, no nothing like that. Well; it was silly really, I wasn't watching where I was walking and fell.'

'I can feel compensation setting in here. Where did you fall?' enquired Alice.

'On South Street,' Joyce replied.

'Hey, I broke my leg on South Street!' interjected Betty with glee, 'Is that the one near Belmont Street?'

'Yes that's right. Did you trip on that open inspection hole?'

'Yes I did! I'm thinking I should complain to the Council, especially as there are now two of us. Do you live nearby?' asked Betty while Alice and the rest listened with excitement as they, in true fortune telling perception, understood which way this conversation was going.

'Yes,' replied Joyce, 'just a couple of miles from South Street.'

'Excuse me for asking,' said Joyce, 'But do you attend the church near there?'

'You mean the spiritualist church on Belmont Street?'

'Yes that's the one. I had just come from there when this happened,' said Joyce.

'Me too!' exclaimed Betty.

'Dangerous place to be,' muttered Alice.

Ignoring Alice, Joyce continued, 'I had just been to a meeting there and was on my way to catch a bus. I thought you looked familiar, maybe we've seen each other in passing at the church before.'

'Yes but it's strange that we should both attend the same church, each break a leg and both end up in the same ward,' exclaimed Betty.

'I know. Plus I was forewarned something like this might happen,' said Joyce.

'How's that?' asked Betty.

'Well you know the man who runs the church?'

'Yes.'

'Well he told me he had foreseen I would meet my twin in destiny. Wonder if he meant you and me?' suggested Joyce.

'That's weird,' said Betty, 'He said almost the same thing to me and here we are.'

'Very strange,' concluded Joyce.

'Strange indeed,' replied Betty.

'I bet the bugger opened the access hole himself,' muttered Alice unsympathetically, 'Good publicity.'

'Hindsight is always more reliable than foresight,' commented another patient.

'Coincidence,' stated an obvious unbeliever in the ward.

'A pure act of God,' said another.

'Lazy workmen more like,' mumbled Alice, 'Still; it's bad news for a church that professes clairvoyance. Two people who attend the same spiritualist church tripping on the same inspection cover, on the same day and end up in the same hospital and on the same ward. Man! That's Karma!'

'I've just thought of something,' continued Alice, 'Why wasn't the cover replaced on the hole after you'd fallen in it Betty? Surely who ever helped you get to hospital would have replaced the damn thing?'

'To be honest I never gave it a moments thought. I was in too much pain at the time to worry about the ill fitting cover. Obviously the ambulance men didn't consider it either. I'm so sorry Joyce, if I had asked them to replace the cover properly, you wouldn't have fallen,' finished Betty in an apologetic tone.

'That's OK, I'm sure you had other things on your mind at the time. In fact I don't know if the cover was replaced after I'd fallen down it,' replied Joyce.

'Some one must have replaced it by now, don't you think?' enquired Alice, 'where was this open cover exactly?'

'On South Street,' replied Betty and Joyce in unison.

'Well correct me if I'm wrong, but isn't there a Catholic church on South Street?' asked Alice.

'Yes, I believe there is,' replied Betty.

'Ahh. I see! Now I understand what's going on . . . That's very sneaky,' muttered Alice.

'I'm following you,' sniggered June from the bed beside Alice.

'Yep! Me too,' contributed another patient with a grin.

'What do you mean? What's going on?' pleaded Betty.

'It's simple really,' laughed Alice.

'What is?' asked Betty.

'What are you talking about?' asked Joyce.

'Well think about it. A manhole cover on the same street as a Catholic church is removed on the route to your Spiritualist church. Don't you see now?' laughed a delighted Alice.

'No!' came the joint reply.

'It's a Catholic ambush!'

On that very improbable statement, a doctor entered the ward, approached Alice and informed her she was to be discharged earlier than anticipated as she now appeared recovered enough to be sent home.

'That's fine by me,' replied Alice, 'but what's the rush?'

'We have to find a bed for another patient who has just come up from A&E,' he explained, 'I'm not sure what's going on today but we've just had another woman brought in with a broken leg!'

With a huge grin Alice quickly began dressing and packing, texting her husband whilst grabbing and folding night clothes and slippers.

'There you go,' she chuckled to the ward in general, 'Ambush!'

Strange events . . . . . *two*.

Again my friend Alice found herself in hospital and she was by now well aware of the routine followed by nurses and doctors in that particular establishment. She was to be admitted into a general medical ward but just for tests this time; she was not poorly and so was in good spirits. Alice knew the ward where she was destined, it had beds for twelve patients; and was normally a friendly environment with much laughter and chat. Alice got on well with both staff and other patients and looked forward to the added bonus of there being a couple of nurses she loved to wind up when ever possible. When well, Alice was quite a joker and most of the staff knew this from her previous hospital stays. But Alice's humour took many forms and this time it bordered on the strange, unlike the amusing quips or jokes she was renowned for.

Her appointment was not until late morning but due to transport issues, Alice had arrived at the hospital much earlier than necessary rather than risk being late and missing her scheduled time. She knew she would have to wait months for another opening. Resigning herself to a long boring wait, Alice decided to head for the hospital café to purchase a coffee and maybe a cream bun – or two. Her recent diet could hang for now, no real point in trying to diet in hospital when the only real pleasure and entertainment is eating. To be honest, Alice never actually dieted as she had no real reason to. But she liked to pretend just to annoy those larger people who claimed to live on diets, while stuffing chocolates and pastries into their ever open mouths.

Alice was aware of the mealtime routines and therefore knew what time lunch was served on the ward. Her appointment was due well before lunch time but understanding the haphazard time table kept by most wards due to the uncertainty of patients conditions, she realised she could be waiting quite a while past the designated time.

Alice was what could be described as a slim woman, standing at only five foot and a Nat's whisker tall and showing little visible signs of her constant illness. Short dark brown hair cropped round her thin face just above her narrow shoulders which were dressed in a blue cardigan covering a white blouse above a knee length plated skirt. Due to her diminished figure and unobtrusive attire, Alice was barely noticed in a crowd. Unless one looked closer at the sparkling eyes and ready to smile mouth. In her mid fifties, Alice had been ill much of her life and the strain was often evident; however her unquenchable spirit and strength could not be deigned. Alice faced life straight on and lived it as full as she could.

While sipping her coffee and munching one of the two cream buns she had chosen from the cake shelve, a familiar voice interrupted her quiet contemplation of the forthcoming events.

'Hi,' came a voice Alice recognised, 'Hi, what are you doing here?'

Looking up from her coffee, Alice saw her friend Jill making a bee line for her table. Alice had known Jill for some time and had often shared a hospital ward with her in the past.

Jill Broadsmith was the opposite of Alice, a large noisy woman with curly fair hair and a round wide face that matched the proportions of her body. Jill was dressed in night clothes and a pink night gown while fluffy slippers slapped the floor as she walked. A white band round her left wrist signified she was a patient, thus making her attire acceptable to all who wondered about this large round apparition that charged through the café, bouncing unsuspecting passersby aside without a care.

'Oh. Hi Jill. You in again?' asked Alice as the human cannon ball reached her table and flopped into a vacant seat beside her.

'Well I've been in for a few days but I'm due to be discharged very soon. I'm just waiting for those young doctors to pull their fingers out and let me go. Anyway, why are you here? I hope you're not too ill again?' answered Jill in a burst of volume while eyeing Alice's untouched cream bun.

'I'm just in for tests this time. They don't really know what's wrong this time so they're going to take most of my blood and hitch me up to as many machines as they can. Should be an interesting few days but least on this occasion I'm able to run away if the tests get too scary.'

'Oh that's not too bad then. Let's hope they sort you out and more importantly, let you out again as soon as possible,' replied Jill absently, a trace of dribble trickled down her chins as she gazed longingly at the delicious cream bun patiently awaiting it's fate in front of Alice.

'Can I get you anything Jill?' asked Alice who had not failed to notice the slobbering lust directed at her bun.

'Ho would you mind? I haven't much money with me in here and I'm starving. Can I have a bun like you have and . . er maybe a slice of that gorgeous looking chocolate cake over there please? I'll pay you back when my old man comes to pick me up later, if that's ok?'

'No problem,' replied Alice as she rose from her chair and made her way over the counter to purchase Jill's request. Alice knew what Jill was like and didn't really mind, after all, she could not have Jill starving to death at her café table. With Jill's abundant figure it would take too long!

Returning to her table Alice smiled as Jill's hands stretched out eagerly for the food, not waiting for Alice to sit and place the sweet cakes on the table. Almost immediately Jill had inserted a huge amount of chocolate cake into her cavernous mouth, her eyes closing as she savoured the rich sweetness that burst onto her taste buds, briefly! The next mouthful was already being aimed at her busy mouth with the speed of a bullet. Trying hard not to laugh at the pitiful sight of a woman gorging, Alice carefully placed a desert fork on the table beside Jill's plate.

'What's that for?' enquired Jill through a full mouth.

'It's a cake fork, so you don't get sticky fingers when eating a moist and creamy cake . . . . Oh!' Alice stopped explaining because the large slice of cake had already disappeared.

'Why are you here again Jill? Sorry I forgot to ask,' said a bemused Alice as the cream bun was now swiftly vanishing down the same destination as the cake.

'Er . . hump . . Sorry, had a mouth full,' apologised Jill while stating the obvious, 'I've had a spot of trouble with my breathing again. The doctors keep telling me it's because I'm over weight. Never heard such rubbish! I'm simply a stout person with big bones. I'm not over weight.' gasped Jill as the last morsel of bun was forced down her ample throat.

'Of course you're not,' agreed Alice with a stifled laugh, 'What can they be thinking?'

'I know! I think I have asthma or something like that. How can weight make breathing difficult? Silly young doctors don't know what they're talking about. Wish I could afford to go private like Mrs Goldsmith, she is covered by burpa you know.'

'I think you mean BUPA?'

'Well yes; what ever. Least those posh doctors there wouldn't tell me I'm fat.'

'Never mind,' said Alice, bored now with the excuses of someone plainly in denial, 'So I assume you're feeling better if you're being discharged today?'

'Yes, just as soon as I get my doctors letter and my medication. My old man is waiting for me to text him with a time of discharge. At the rate they're going, it could be tomorrow!'

'So what ward are you on this time?' asked Alice.

'I'm on Napoleon ward, bay C,' answered Jill while dabbing at her mouth in case she had missed a morsel of cake.

'Ha; that's interesting. What bed are you in?'

'Dunno why you're so interested, but I'm in bed 6, but hopefully not for much longer. I suppose, saying that, I had better head back and see if those doctors have woken up yet,' said Jill as she rose like a mountain from her chair.

'Sorry Jill, but do you know if anyone else is being discharged from your ward today?'

Jill smiled, the faint light of understanding appearing in her eyes. 'Nope; you're ok, I'm the only one going out today. What's on your mind this time? What are you planning?'

'Ho nothing,' replied Alice with a grin, 'I just like to know where I stand when I finally get called in. Anyway, it's been lovely to see you again, make sure you stay well this time.'

'Yes it was nice to see you again as well. I hope your tests work out OK and I'll try not to hold your bed up too long. In fact I think I'll go have a word with that doctor now, and tell him to get a move on.'

With that Jill left the café and waddled off back to her ward, leaving Alice musing on the high cost of coffee these days, high when Jill is around anyway. Alice ordered another coffee and sat back in the warm sunshine streaming in through the large window beside her table. Her gaze followed the comings and goings of all the people around her, patients nipping outside for a quick smoke, doctors joining them. Visitors and outpatients heading to and from their destinations, and multitudes of administrators and managers swarmed along the corridors, papers and files gripped tightly in their hands as they hurried about in a vain attempt to appear busy.

Eventually Alice was called to her ward, a trainee nurse locating her still in the café and led the way along the corridors and into a lift that carried them to the required floor and ward. Although the nurse was only trying to be helpful, Alice knew the way from experience, many experiences actually. But she decided not to undermine the youthful and confident spirit of the nurse in front, and followed dutifully behind.

Upon reaching the bay that was to be her home for the next few days, Alice paused and with exaggerated movements, lifted her right hand to her brow while appearing to steady herself against the wall with her left.

'Are you alright?' asked the trainee nurse.

'Yes I think so,' replied Alice with a loud sigh, 'I just have this strange feeling that someone is talking to me. But never mind, once I reach my bed I'll be fine.'

'Here you are then,' said the nurse, 'this is your bed, do you need any help getting undressed and into the bed? . . . . What's the matter? Are you feeling OK?' finished the nurse in a concerned voice.

Alice had walked slowly up to the designated bed, placed one hand on it and jerked in back as if she had been burnt and then began to sway.

'I do feel slightly weird,' whispered Alice, 'Perhaps you'd better get one of the staff nurses, just in case?'

The trainee hurried from the ward, a look of concern on her face and with urgency in her steps. The rest of the patients in the bay watched with delight, this was an unexpected source of entertainment and should be devoured to its fullest possibility. With all eyes on her, Alice simply stood beside her bed and waited to see which of the duty staff was to be her victim. She hoped it would be one of the regular staff, but in truth she did not mind. Alice had a plan and she was going to see it through. Alice was still swaying gently as the trainee re-entered the bay with a senior nurse in tow.

'Hello Alice,' said a small blond staff nurse who obviously recognised her, 'What's the matter? I though you were just in for tests?'

Alice moaned and swayed, reaching out she placed one hand back onto the bed, placing the back of her other hand against her forehead.

'I'm getting a name,' she wailed with eyes rolling, 'I'm getting someone's name.'

'Who's name? What are you talking about Alice? Are you feeling OK?' asked the staff nurse.

'Ooooo I'm getting a name . . . .,' repeated Alice with more moans, groans and increasing active swaying, 'I'm getting a name, calling me, calling to me from this bed.'

'What?' demanded the shocked trainee.

'What is the matter with you? And what name are you on about? Don't you think you should sit down? You're swaying so much I'm afraid you may fall down,' implored the staff nurse, now with a disturbed expression.

'Oooo . . . I'm getting a name . . . Jill, I think the name I'm getting from this bed is Jill,' moaned Alice overdramatically.

Alice allowed herself to sway nearer the bedside chair before exaggerating a swoon and flopping heavily into it. Still gently moaning, Alice swivelled her eyes wildly and fanned herself with one hand.

'Oooo I must be sidekick,' muttered Alice.

'I think you mean psychic,' corrected the trainee.

'She's not psychic!' said the staff nurse, 'OK, Jill who? We get lots of Jill's through this ward, so try to be a little more defined please.'

'Ooooo I'm getting a name . . . .!'

'Yes we know that.'

'Ooooo I'm getting a name, Jill . . . . Jill Broadsmith I think. Oooo what's happening to me?' cried Alice.

At this statement the trainee blanched and very nearly jumped from her skin. Several of the watching patients dived beneath their bedclothes, while others made the sign of the cross furiously over their chests. One patient quickly reached for her bed pan, the strain obviously too much for her bladder.

'Ere, she was in that bed, there was a Jill Broadsmith in that bed, she was only discharged today. That woman must be psychic,' enjoined one of the watching patients as her own astonishment forced her to interject.

'That's right,' said the trainee.

'What, the large woman discharged an hour ago?' asked an incredulous staff nurse.

'Ooooo . . . .'

'Yes Mrs Jillian Broadsmith came in for a few days with breathing difficulties,' answered the trainee.

'Oooooo . . . .'

'Shut up please Alice! So how come you know this person was in this bed before you?' demanded a disturbed and slightly angry staff nurse.

'Oooooo! I don't know who you're all talking about. I'm only getting a name . . . Oooo.'

'Blimey!' said the staff nurse, 'perhaps she is psychic. But I don't think so really!' she finished with a mutter.

'I think so,' said the trainee, 'it's quite frightening really.'

'Ooooooo! . . . . . I'm seeing things now!' cried Alice with lots of theatrical hand waving and eye swivelling, 'I can see a large woman, a big woman who is telling me her name is Jill.'

'Here! This is getting creepy,' muttered another patient.

'Bloody weird is what it is,' stated yet another.

'OK Alice, try to calm down now. We'll get you a cup of tea, have you had anything to eat yet?' asked the staff nurse in an attempt to gain control of the situation.

'Ooooo! . .. oo a cuppa would be lovely,' said Alice, 'And no I've not had any lunch yet. If you would be so kind? I'm feeling so exhausted by all this, I could eat a horse.'

'That's fine then, we'll get you a drink and some lunch. You just rest and try to relax.'

Both nurses quickly left the room, the trainee obviously now a believer and the staff nurse shocked but suspicious; both eager to pass on these strange happenings to their colleagues.

The trainee returned just moments later with a steaming cup of tea and a plate of food she had sent up from the hospital kitchen. Alice tucked in eagerly, ignoring the staring eyes and whispered mutterings around her. Several times as she was eating, other members of staff peered into the ward at her before rushing off to update their colleagues. Alice could hear the gossip flying across the corridor as speculation increased in intensity as everyone attempted to explain Alice's psychic moment. So far none of the other patients had spoken to her; in fact most had hardly spoken at all. The thoughts of each one ranged far across the spectrum of the afterlife, clairvoyance and the supernatural, everyone waiting with glee to announce this strange event to loved ones, friends and general passers by when the imminent visiting time arrived.

Alice finished her meal and relaxed back into the chair, a high backed arm chair of the type commonly used in many hospitals, and eventually nodded off. Some time later her doze was disturbed by the excited buzz of visiting time. Although she was only in for tests, Alice was expecting a visit from her husband and began straightening her clothes and patting her hair into place in readiness. Ten minutes into visiting hour her husband strode in. Like Alice he was very familiar with the hospital, many of the wards and most of the regular staff. He had been visiting or accompanying Alice through various hospitals ever since they married and took little notice of the surroundings or other patients, no matter how injured or sick they appeared. Walking straight to her bedside, Alice's husband planted a kiss on her cheek and began the monotonous idle conversations that all regular patients have with their long suffering spouses.

Barely had the initial required items of chat concluded when the staff nurse came up to Alice's bed. The staff nurse was well known to both Alice and her husband so it was not unusual for her to stop by for a few words with both of them. By now of course, Alice was showing no signs of the earlier performance, sitting straight in her chair with a cheerful smile on her face as she greeted the still concerned staff nurse.

'Hello Kay,' said Alice's husband first, 'Nice to see you again, though it would have been even better if we didn't keep meeting in here.'

'Hi John, I hope you've been keeping an eye on her at home these days? Actually you haven't noticed anything strange about her behaviour recently have you?' asked Kay, the staff nurse.

'No, nothing apart from her normal oddities,' smiled John.

'Thanks a bunch!' interrupted Alice; 'You wait till we get home,' she finished with a laugh.

'Why? What's she been up to now?' enquired John.

'It seems your wife may be something of a clairvoyant.'

'What?'

'Well we had a small episode earlier when she was first admitted.'

'Do tell,' said Alice's husband while casting suspicious glances at his so innocent wife.

'Well when she came in, it appears she heard a voice telling her who the previous occupant of this bed was.'

'Did she saw who it was?'

'Yes, she said, and rightly so, that it was a woman named Jillian Broadsmith. Have you heard that name before?'

Suddenly nurse Kay noticed a wide grin spreading across the face of Alice while her husband began chuckling. Still very bemused, Kay did not pick up on this significance as she repeated, 'Maybe you know the name Jill. Does that ring a bell?'

'Ho yes. Alice and Jill have known each other for many years,' laughed the husband, 'don't know how she knew Jill had been in here before her though.'

'Oh didn't I tell you?' Alice asked innocently of an increasingly red faced nurse, 'Jill and I met for coffee in the hospital café just before she was discharged.'

'Well you bloody . . . . .!' raged nurse Kay seconds before the humour of the situation hit her.

'Gotcha!' laughed Alice.

Chapter Twelve: The Condiments Man.

It is a fact that most people frequently lament about the terrible school dinners they suffered as a child, it is also a fact that hospital food seldom escapes this form of criticism either. Patients young, old, fat and thin bemoan the quality and quantity of meals served by hospital kitchens or contracted caterers.

In the UK the standard of cuisine can be quite good but earning appreciation for a well presented, planned and enjoyable meal can be harder to achieve than flying to the moon. The problem begins with the patients; as usual it is all their fault, someone once said hospitals would work brilliantly if not for the patients. Most people have the good fortune not to endure a stay as an inpatient too often in their otherwise healthy lives, thus it can come as quite a shock, firstly to find themselves in hospital and secondly, eating food that is certainly not like mummy used to cook.

Personally I have no such qualms about hospital food as I spent much of my youth in boarding schools where food of any shape, taste or appearance was valued higher than gold. Remember I was a child at the time and gold held little interest for me anyway, but food was an entirely different issue. A boarding school pupil is always hungry! Quickly I developed an iron stomach and a virtually insatiable appetite as my initial route to survival, being a fussy eater was definitely not on my menu. If the food was reasonably hot, only green where it should be green and any livestock involved was actually dead and not still crawling around the plate, then I would eat it. Except celery, I hate celery with a passion!

The modern westernised inhabitant of our planet in the twenty-first century will have different views on what is considered *fine* food. Most enjoy the good fortune to have home cooked meals on at least a daily basis, whether prepared by their own fair hand or dished up by a parent or partner or spouse. After such a persistent daily routine, each and every one of us develops our own personal tastes, choices of foods and cooking methods. Even those who cannot cook or will not cook still have their favourites between fast foods such as an Indian curry, Chinese take-a-way; MacDonald's, Burger King or Fish & Chips. If this freedom of choice is suddenly snatched from our hungry little hands, many of us simply cannot cope and immediately begin complaining and carping about the unsatisfactory nourishment served in such a bewildering establishment as a hospital.

I had long grown used to my fellow patients showing varying degrees of horror or hunger when presented with their meal tray, and was prepared for the usual grumbles, exclamations of pleasure or disgust, and occasionally a patients rapid flight to the nearest toilet, solely inspired by the sight of the culinary delight placed in front of him. Occasionally I personally still encounter the odd culinary surprise.

Something different occurred on this particular incarceration into the local medical motel that I had not encountered before. In the bed beside mine was a mature gentleman who loved his food. He had no qualms about hospital cuisine at all, in fact he freely admitted to relishing every meal, a statement that caused some disbelief amongst a couple of fellow patients. I admit to pondering the standard of food he received at home if he considered the mass produced National Health Service nutrition with such acclaimed favour, but I refrained from asking. As already mentioned, I have no concerns with the quality of sustenance served on a hospital ward, but not even I would admit to relishing each meal with such gusto!

It was evident that he loved his food and it appeared even the food based products supplied via the huge hospital kitchens. Each day he would carefully examine his menu, ticking off the items he wanted with anticipation of a wholesome and tasty meal ahead of him.

It was soon noticed that he favoured the traditional fare, roast pork or beef, pies, sausages or casseroles. He was less keen on pasta based recipes, rice dishes or in his opinion, any food with unpronounceable foreign names, like curry or pizza. And so it was with delight that he discovered roast beef and Yorkshire pudding heading the list of available meals on his menu for Sunday. With glee he carefully ticked all the main ingredients of a traditional Sunday roast. Beef, Yorkshires, turnip, peas, roast potatoes and gravy. One could almost hear him salivating over the prospect of such a meal, although he was somewhat disappointed that the offered deserts did not include apple pie and custard, so he reluctantly chose a trifle as a weak substitute.

The next day arrived and the patient eagerly wolfed down breakfast, undertook his ablutions, achieved his morning walk along the corridors of magical modern marvellous medicine, read his daily paper and performed all the tasks expected of a hospital patient. At last the hour arrived and the heated lunch trolley could be heard clattering its way to our ward. In the constant tedium of being confined in hospital, meal times take on the status of an interesting interlude in the continuing boredom. So all the patients began to ready themselves for the meal, hungry or not, it did not matter, it was simply a break in the otherwise repetitive routine of the day. The meal duly arrived and we set about munching our way through the mass produced, precooked and transported food. I too had ordered the roast beef, but as an experienced patient I knew what to expect.

Next to me my fellow patient's eagerly awaited meal was placed in front of my neighbouring patient. He gazed loving down at his plate, grasped his knife and fork, and stopped!

'Excuse me?' he called to the nurse as she headed off to collect the next lunch tray, 'Could I trouble you for some mustard please? English if possible?'

'Pardon?' replied the nurse with furrowed brow.

'Sorry, but could I have some mustard?' requested the patient.

'Oh. We don't have any mustard, only salt, pepper and red or brown sauce. Sorry,' And with a rustle of her plastic apron she left to continue her duties.

I had been obviously listening to this exchange; the other chap was only a few feet away so in truth I could not avoid it. As I watched, his face fell with utter disappointment.

'No mustard,' he muttered down at his plate, 'Roast beef with no mustard!'

I really thought he was about to cry. All the other patients including myself were happily or otherwise stuffing the food into our faces without a single care or thought about mustard, while throwing occasional glances towards the distraught patient as he remained staring at his plate. Finally just as we thought he would refuse the meal, he shrugged his shoulders and began to eat, though muttering his displeasure throughout the meal.

Over the few days of our stay in the medical establishment, his interest and fondness for hospital food began to rapidly dissipate. Roast pork arrived with no apple sauce, roast chicken was presented with no bread sauce, sausages remained unaccompanied by a dollop of mustard on the plate and his dejection was complete when he was served roast lamb, with no mint sauce!

After what seemed a life time, my discharge was imminent and I eagerly awaited my release from the monotonous discomfort and imprisonment of the hospital. I was lucky for none of the other patients had been successful in their efforts to escape and would remain in captivity for at least another day. This included my now totally defeated neighbour. His whole attitude towards food had undergone a complete change, no longer did he rave about the listed menu items with such anticipation or delight, nor did he show the same level of enthusiasm at the approach of each meal, it was sad to behold. His health improved but his spirit was broken! We all worried for him in case the decline in his attitude towards his beloved food began to take a toll on his medical condition. The true traditional English gent had been forced to his knees by the simple lack of expected culinary condiments to accompany his own traditional nutritional desires.

I was sad to see the chap in such a state, he was very likable, polite and well spoken. He had welcomed me upon my arrival into the ward and offered help and support during my initial days of suffering. But I could think of no way to return his generous and caring nature as I began to pack my bags in readiness of freedom.

'Here you go,' said one of the nurses as she strode into the ward clutching a paper bag, 'Maybe this will cheer you up?'

'What?' exclaimed my startled neighbour as the paper bag was thrust into his hands.

'We noticed how upset you've been lately so the staff have prescribed you something to help. Enjoy!' said the nurse as she smiled happily and left the confused patient still sat with a paper bag in his hands.

Mystified, my neighbour cautiously opened the bag and peered inside. Suddenly a huge grin erupted across his face. A whoop of delight escaped his lips as the contents of the bag became apparent. With shaking fingers he began pulling items out and laying them carefully on his bedside table. First to emerge was a small jar of English mustard, followed closely by a jar of mint sauce and a jar of apple sauce. Then came a tiny sample jar of pickle, a jar of horseradish sauce, a small jar of cranberry was produced and finally two packets containing bread and tartar sauce that simply required the addition of hot water joined the array of condiments on his table. There was even a small squeezy bottle of onion relish nestling amongst the unexpected gifts.

As I grasped my bags and offered goodbyes and good luck to all the patients in the ward, my eyes almost filled with tears as the last patient I offered my farewell to was now one of the happiest men alive!

Alien Substance.

In one particular hospital each patient receives a menu for the following day's lunch and supper, which is duly filled in though often with no idea what one is actually ordering. I believe this is the usual procedure for most hospital today but I cannot verify this fact so I will comment only on this one hospital's culinary methods. And surprises.

In a small effort to combat some of the tedium experienced as a recovering patient, I had several years before began playing a little game, or perhaps setting myself a challenge would be a more apt description. Each day upon receiving the offered menu I always select the option of a milk based pudding for the following day's supper desert. This is not because I especially like milk based puddings; it was more the case that I enjoy surprises. Described on the menu as rice pudding, tapioca, semolina, ground rice; sago or macaroni, at least one of these deserts was included on the menu each day as they are considered easy to devour, healthy and unlikely to disturb a weakened digestive system. An added factor when forming menus for the sick and elderly, is that milk puddings do not require the assistance of teeth!

Every day during my multitude of medical imprisonments, I tick the option of a milk based pudding no matter what its description, be it rice, tapioca or sago, I really do not mind. The reason I chose the milk pudding is purely the anticipation of the surprise when it actually turns up on my tray. Over the years this has been a constant source of amusement to me as I gently lift the cover off the bowl containing the pudding and examine it closely. The entertainment is achieved by attempting to identify exactly which of the puddings has arrived. I may have ordered semolina but this does not ensure I will get semolina. It appears that although the item listed on the menu has a description, the substance in the bowl often bares no resemblance at all.

Yes it is a milk based pudding, but which one is the question that must be answered, visual indication is insufficient, they each have the same lumpy milk appearance so taste is the final decider. One or sometimes two mouthfuls will frequently identify the offered desert as rice rather than the sago requested, however on occasion even taste fails to recognise the origins of the dish, and periodically I simply cannot give a description or name to the desert staring back at me from its bowl!

So my little nightly gastronomic guessing game revolves around using my limited culinary skills to place a correct, or in most cases, an approximate label of identification upon the milky, gooey desert sitting patiently in a bowl on my meal tray. Such is the tedium of a hospital ward during the final stages of recovery. Sad!

I must state that the outcome of a pudding identification is not really important; I do not care what the substance may be as long as it is edible. It is the small entertainment value that gives the most pleasure. Unfortunately on several occasions even this has not been the case. It has been known for an alleged milk pudding to resemble wall paper paste and taste just as pleasant. But it is not only the milk puddings that have required close scrutiny over the past few years; the soups entitled Chefs Own Recipe have also raised doubts as to the correct identification. One recently served soup was actually cut into slices before being placed on the unsuspecting patient's plate. I remember on that occasion, I spread my *soup* on a piece of bread and butter and greatly enjoyed my sandwich!

But the one food item on the menu of many hospitals that I avoid at all costs to health and sanity is the fish cake! Never, ever again!

Chapter Thirteen: Rapid Discharge.

One morning, just after breakfast and before the nurses arrived in gangs to drag us from our warm beds and usher the more capable ones amongst us off to the shower room, something happened I had never seen before in this particular hospital. An elderly man, still dressed in hat and coat, walked into our ward accompanied by a trainee nurse and made his way to an empty bed in the corner by the door. The new patient was quite elderly, appearing to be in his eighties and looking very confused and bewildered at this strange turn of events. The nurse then instructed him in what to do next, but failed to check he actually understood. She dropped his bag onto the floor beside his bed and then promptly left him standing alone in a ward full of strange men and with no idea as to why he was there.

    With a loud sigh he eyed up the crisp clean bed that awaited him. Following a period of pondering he eventually arrived at the conclusion that he should get into the bed beside were he stood. With some effort he picked up the bag from the floor and placed it on the bed, it appeared to be an overnight bag. Still standing, he glanced round the room at us, we were actively staring back at him, wondering what he was doing and if there was going to be any entertainment.

    'Mornin' mate,' said one of the patients, 'Are you OK?'

    'I think so,' replied the stranger, 'I've come in for what they call a procedure I think. I've been waiting for two years then suddenly I get a phone call asking me to come into the hospital as a bed is available. Not sure what it's all about but the nurse who met me told me to come in here and get into bed, can't understand that, going to back to bed in the morning. My name is Tom by the way, nice to meet you all.'

    'You too Tom. What's the procedure?' I asked.

'Dunno really, my daughter normally handles things for me, I live alone you know and she pops in every day to check I'm alright and sort things out for me.'

'So you don't know why you're here?' I continued, incredulously.

'No, not really,' said Tom, 'I was quite ill sometime ago but I thought that was all fixed. Wonder where my daughter is?'

'She'll probably be in to see you later, during visiting time.'

'Oh; that's good. Why do I have to go to bed? I don't normally go to bed during the day.'

With that the new patient began reluctantly readying himself for bed. Tom appeared frail, a bald head with just a few wisps of hair over his ears, small glasses resting precariously on his thin hooked nose. His clothes seemed a couple of sizes too large for him and he had some difficulty in manoeuvring his overnight bag. Sloping shoulders and a weary expression confirmed his long years and portrayed a resignation that accompanies those who have seen much, done much and are now tired.

As he began to undress, we suggested he pull the bed curtains around to protect his decency, and our stomachs. We had not long had breakfast and an old, thin man undressing in front of us was not something we wished to see! It was soon evident that the poor chap was very frail indeed as the curtains proved too much for him. Noticing the new inmate's difficulties the guy in the next bed gallantly stepped forward to help. This small act of assistance was obviously appreciated by Tom and his facial expression suggested this simple act would fill even the greatest cynic with restored faith in humanity. The patient, who volunteered his help, actually needed help himself. Attached to wires connected to monitors, tubes connected to intravenous drips and still poorly enough to be almost as frail as the gent he was attempting to help! I could not stand this pitiful scenario any longer and as I was fractionally fitter and certainly younger than the majority of the ward, I slowly fell from my bed, promptly landed flat on my face, perhaps not so much fitter after all. Embarrassed but not injured, I inched carefully onto my feet and staggered over to pull the curtains for them, before the curtains won the fight and caused injury to the two patients with a vicious attack of hanging cloth!

With curtains drawn to protect his decency the new guy proceeded to undress. We knew this little detail because we could all hear the huffs, puffs and groans that accompanied the sounds of laces being untied, fumbled zips and the rustling of clothing. Me and the other volunteer made our way slowly and carefully back to the sanctuary of our own beds and flopped, exhausted by the almost impossible battle with flowered bed curtains.

'OK I'm done, can you help me pull back the curtains please?' came a voice from behind the curtain screen.

'Ring your nurse call bell please Tom, the big orange button on the handset on your bedside table. Sorry,' I replied to his plea between gasping for breath as I lay like a horizontal statue on my bed.

'Oh; OK,' answered Tom before a crash indicated he had dropped the handset on the floor.

'Oh!'

'NURSE!' shouted several voices in unison.

Moments later and to our combined relief a very sexy nurse wiggled into the ward and enquired what the noise was all about. The initial volunteer took it upon himself to explain, trying hard to retain some small aspect of his masculinity as he admitted none of us were capable of drawing the curtains from around the new guy's bed. She smiled, a knowing smile that told us all that no matter how much we flirted with her, no matter how many lurid suggestions we may make, she knew she was perfectly safe from we ill and knackered old men. Ashamed we cast our eyes to the floor in embarrassment and sorrow, we also knew we were no threat and our egos suffered a mighty blow. As if to tease us further, the shapely and attractive young girl seductively dressed in a nurse's uniform wiggled sexily as she slowly drew back the curtains. Obviously enjoying our distress the nurse then bent slowly at the waist as she leaned down, her perfect bottom displayed to all, and with exaggerated care, repositioned Tom's shoes under his bed, before leaving the ward with another wiggle of her hips.

'No fair! Do it again please?'

'That's not nice.'

'Careful, one day I'll befit again.'

'Come back! I need my curtains drawn.'

These and other cries and suggestions accompanied the delightful tease as she departed while one or two elderly right hands rapidly disappeared beneath bed covers.

By now Tom had donned his pyjamas and made himself comfortable in bed, though the way he was stretched out and lying so quiet and still, had me worried until he spoke, muttering to himself actually, not the rest of us. With the mental picture of the young nurse still fresh in our minds, no one spoke for several minutes, but eventually curiosity reared its head.

'So why are you here Tom? I mean, what's wrong with you?' one of the patients enquired.

'Dunno really. I didn't understand when I was first told, I'm even more uncertain now,' Tom replied.

'Well, is it your heart? Your lungs? Or the big C, if you don't mind me asking? Have you got a broken leg? Surely you must have some idea of what's up with you?' asked the patient persistently.

'I really don't know,' stated Tom, 'in fact I don't think I should be in here at all. I'm just taking up a bed that someone else may need. I wish I was home.'

'I think you'd know if it was a broken leg,' laughed the patient.

'Hang on, I'll check,' said Tom before lifting one leg after the other under his bed covers.

'Nope. My legs seem fine so it can't be them.'

'Oh that's good,' joked the talkative patient.

'Hasn't anyone told you what's going on?' I asked.

'No. Well maybe. They talked at me a lot, but they kept using words I didn't understand. I got fed up after a while and turned my hearing aid off, they all looked like fish out of water with their mouths opening and closing without any sound. Anyway my daughter understands what they're jabbering on about.'

'Do you feel poorly then Tom?'

'Nope. Feel right as rain. Don't know why I'm here. Don't know why I have to be in bed, don't go to bed during the day at home,' moaned Tom.

'You know you're now in hospital don't you Tom?'

'Of course I know I'm in hospital! I just don't know why I have to be in bed.'

'That's what happens in hospitals Tom; they put you in bed so it's easier for the doctors to examine you. They may let you get up afterwards, if you're lucky.'

'Oh good. Don't like being in bed during the day.'

'Yep, we gathered that Tom. Just be patient . . . oops, pardon the pun. Wait till you've seen a doctor and then you'll know more. Well perhaps you won't because you don't listen to them, so we'll listen and let you know what's happening. Is that OK?'

'Yes that would be fine. Where are all the doctors anyway? I haven't seen a single one since I've been here.'

'Have you seen several scruffy young men hanging around the nurses?'

'Yes I've seen those, wondered who they were.'

'That's the doctors these days I'm afraid. They don't wear white coats or suits anymore.'

'Scruffy buggers!' said Tom.

Just as Tom ended his comment, two men entered the ward and stood beside Tom's bed, peering at a folder full of the gibberish commonly known as doctors hand writing. The older and slightly smarter dressed man spoke first and introduced himself as the ward consultant. He spoke quietly to Tom as he began his examination with a stethoscope on Tom's chest; he then checked Tom's pulse before stepping back, apparently satisfied with his investigations. It was obvious the consultant was unaware of Tom's reasons for being in hospital as he constantly referred to the medical records. It was apparent he considered Tom as routine, the ward consultant was simply doing his morning rounds to check we were all actually still alive and breathing. Later in the morning our own consultants and doctors would arrive and examine us properly and decide on the appropriate course of treatment, but for now the ward consultant was in charge.

This consultant himself appeared near to retirement age, and it was not an easy task overseeing several wards with only the notes from other doctors to guide him in each patient's condition. A ward consultant can be in charge of several wards in a department, but is normally only on duty to cover emergencies until his golf playing colleagues returned to work. So this particular consultant had no prior knowledge of Tom, all the consultant saw was an elderly gentleman with no apparent illness, disease, missing limbs or bloodstained sheets. It was also the job requirement of the consultant to free up any beds that could be used for another patient and allow him to reach the government targets of the day.

Government targets have long been the scourge of hospitals and schools alike. Some junior government officials or politicians with an eye on building a reputation deciding that hospitals should treat more patients in a shorter period of time. Thus the emphasise fell on senior doctors to get patients treated and discharged as soon as medically possible, and sometimes even when it was not!

'How have you been lately Mr Tregonning?' enquired the consultant.

'I'm fine doctor,' replied Tom, 'in fact I've been well for some time, apart from getting old of course.'

'Do you feel well enough to go home?'

'Yes I do, I'd love to be allowed home.'

'Do you have someone to look after you at home Mr Tregonning?'

'Yes, my daughter takes care of me, shopping and stuff like that. No problems there.'

'Right then, we'll let you go home today and arrange an immediate appointment with your GP. Is that alright with you?'

'That's lovely doctor, thank you very much. Can I go right away?'

'I don't see why not. Can you get home by yourself or do you need hospital transport?'

'No I'm fine doctor, I'll ring my daughter and she'll pick me up.'

'Well nice to have met you Mr Tregonning, hopefully you'll start to feel much better now.'

'Thank you doctor.'

Both doctors immediately left the room, the consultant and his silent shadow. Tom was delighted, we were astounded! What had just happened? With a massive grin on his face, Tom rose quickly from the bed, quick for a fail elderly man that is, and reached for his clothes.

'Don't worry about the curtains gents,' he said, 'I always keep my underwear on when in a strange place. And it's clean. I don't wish to embarrass myself anymore than age has already done.'

Shaky and excited hands fumbled with clothes before pyjamas were stuffed unceremoniously into the overnight bag. Within moments he was dressed, packed and ready to go.

'Well goodbye everyone.' he said, 'Thanks for you help earlier and it's been nice meeting you.'

With those parting words, Tom scampered from the ward with a speed that belied his venerable age. We all looked at each other in confusion and amazement! Tom had been on the ward for less than an hour. Why put someone into a hospital bed for a ten minute examination by a doctor? We were bewildered, but intrigued at what would happen next.

A few minutes later two nurses strode into our ward, one was the sexy one who liked to tease, the other was a Health Care Assistant, know as an HCL. The HCL began rousting us from our warm and comfortable beds and shooed us towards the shower room. The sexy nurse held several forms in her hands and she headed for Tom's now vacant bed.

'Where's Tom?' she enquired of the ward in general.

'He's gone,' was the reply from several of us.

'Gone where?'

'He's gone home as far as we know,' I said.

'What? What do you mean, gone home?'

'Two doctors came in and saw him, then told him he could go home.'

'What the . . . hell is happening?' she demanded as panic lined her face.

Quickly she ran from the room and soon shouts of concern could be heard from the nurse's station. Next the ward manager and senior staff nurse burst into the ward and peered in astonishment at Tom's empty bed. The ward manager examined the bed space for signs of clothing or slippers that might indicate we were winding them up and Tom was actually only in the toilet. Of course they found nothing and exited the ward as quickly as they had entered. Moments later the guilty consultant came in accompanied by the ward manager. They both stared at the dishevelled bed before vanishing out of the door once more. The tease dashed in again, looking very flustered as she too examined the bed space for clues or anything that might suggest Tom was lurking somewhere and had not actually left the hospital. She also found nothing and vacated the ward almost at a run.

The hubble and frantic confusion continued unabated outside our ward while a couple of HCL's proceeded to ensure we were clean and tidy and our beds were remade.

'Well,' I said when we were all finally washed, combed, shaved, tidied and all securely back in our ward.

'What do you make of Tom's rapid discharge?' I asked the ward in general.

'Hehe. Seems he managed to beat the system. I've never seen anyone so eager to leave hospital, but it doesn't make sense, dragging the poor bloke all the way in here for just a few moments with a doctor. I think something's gone wrong, someone has cocked up,' replied the talkative patient with some glee.

'Yeah me too,' came a chorus of agreement from the other patients.

'Wonder what sexy nurse is going to do now?' I wondered.

'Dunno,' pondered the talkative patient, 'Don't really think it was her fault. She may have almost given us heart failure with her arse in the air like that, but she didn't have anything to do with Tom's discharge.'

'Yeah, I nearly had a stroke,' chipped in the guy in the bed next to Tom's vacant bed, 'I say nearly because she was just outta reach!' he laughed.

'Wonder what was wrong with Tom? He didn't have a clue about his own condition and didn't seem to care,' I contributed in a more serious manner.

'Ah; many old people are like that these days,' replied the talkative one, 'They have grown up with authority stuffed down their throats, what with the war and all that. So now they simply sit back and do as they're told, not bothering to concern themselves because they're absolutely convinced the *man* will look after them. If a doctor told them the moon was actually green, they'd believe him!'

'Bugger that,' I retorted, 'I want to know every thing that is happening to me, every thing that's ever happened to me and what will eventually happen to me. Doctors are only human after all, well; most of 'em. Some leave a lot to be desired but that's what makes them human. Buggering things up now and again is normal, everyone does it. It's just that buggering up things when a life is at stake tends to be a tad more important than a mechanic missing a problem with your car.'

'True,' said the talkative one, 'Still, I wonder who messed up with Tom?'

We were soon to find out, and in a strange way we were correct in our presumptions. In any hospital, the same as any venue were many people gather for work, gossip and secrets abound freely. Mid morning and in came the tea trolley, today pushed by a stout but friendly middle aged woman. With a smile for each patient she took our drink orders and served the tea, coffee and hot chocolate, and because she was nice, we even received a biscuit each. As she worked she chatted amiably with us all, joking with those of us she knew from past admissions and offering an appropriate face of sympathy to those who liked to constantly moan about their illness or injury. Eventually she arrived at Tom's empty bed.

'Where this chap?' she questioned, 'I saw him come in this morning.'

'He's gone home,' replied the talkative one.

'Really? I thought he was in for a procedure? Strange he's been discharged so soon.'

'OK, I gotta ask, what's a *procedure*?' I asked her.

'Oh that's just a fancy name for an operation or something like that.'

'Well why don't they just call it an operation?' I said in some confusion.

'It's because they don't want to alarm the patient. Calling it a procedure is easier for many people to cope with, because they don't understand what it means, it's considered better than hearing the frightening word; operation.'

'Ahh!' said I.

'What was his name anyway?' the tea lady enquired.

'Tom Tregonning,' replied the talkative one.

'I wonder if he was related to the chap on the next door male bay?' she asked speculatively, 'we had a chap in there for a couple of days called Tobias Tregonning.'

'So,' I began with seeds of realisation growing in my mind, 'Tom was a Mr T. Tregonning and Tobias was a Mr T. Tregonning?'

'Yes,' responded the tea lady, 'good job they were not both in the same bay. Both in the same ward would be bad enough!'

'What was the problem with Tobias?' asked another patient who had also begun to see the light.

'He had pneumonia I think,' answered the tea lady.

'OK, so he had a chest infection, that's what pneumonia is, isn't it?' enquired the quiet patient.

'Yes, that's right. You could hear him coming down the corridor with his wheezing and coughing,' she replied.

My sudden realisation had obviously hit the quiet patient also. Without another word he looked round at each of us patients, I offered a nod of understanding, some returned blank looks and one had no idea what planet he was on so he did not count. Slowly and mindful of his condition, the quiet patient reached for his nurse call and depressed the large orange button.

Moments later in came our sexy nurse, still looking very flustered because the event with Tom had not yet been explained.

Quickly looking about the room to identify who had called, she saw the illuminated call button beside the quiet patient's bed and moved to him.

'What can I do for you?' she asked, all teasing and flirtation gone for the moment.

'Well I can think of a few things,' smiled the quiet one, 'but it's more of the case of what I can do for you.'

'What are you talking about? I don't have time for games; we're still trying to discover why a patient was discharged so quickly. What do you want?'

'Yes I know, but if we solved the problem, would it earn us some brownie points?'

'Yes maybe, if you're lucky, of course it would,' replied the increasing frustrated nurse.

'OK. That doctor who came and discharged Tom,' he began, 'did he actually pick up the correct medical records for Tom?'

'Or Mr T. Tregonning?' I asked her with a wink at the quiet one across the room.

'Thomas of course,' she retorted, 'the doctor would not be that stupid . . . . . Oh!'

Without another word she virtually ran from the ward, only to reappear a few moments later with the ward consultant, ward manager and senior staff nurse in tow. In her hands the sexy nurse carried two folders containing medical records, both were clearly marked with the name Mr T. Tregonning. Without a word, obviously trying to reduce the doctor's embarrassment, she pointed at one of the files and then indicated the bed number located on the wall behind the bed space.

Each of the individual bays contained in the ward were identified by numbers, each bed within a bay was identified by letters. Tom had been in bed 2A when the ward consultant discharged him.

Attempting to hide his reddening face, the consultant, ward manager and the nurse quietly left the room again.

No sooner then they had exited the ward doors, laughter broke out in the ward, even the tea lady who had watched the exchange joined in, though with surreptitiously glances at the door in case a member of authority entered. It had become evident to all of us that the doctor had picked up the wrong file. Admittedly the records belonging to Tobias Tregonning of bed 2B should have been forwarded to the records department within hours of his discharge, but possibly it was awaiting further information or adjustment. The busy consultant had read Mr T. Tregonning and wrongly assumed the file referred to Mr Thomas Tregonning. No blame could be laid entirely on the consultant; Tom himself was too keen to get home again and gave the doctor no indication that he was actually admitted for a procedure. Thinking he was examining Tobias Tregonning, the doctor had correctly checked his lungs and pulse and had obviously noted his healthy breathing. Under the impression his patient had suffered from pneumonia, the consultant had decided he was now clear and ready for discharge. Tom had not helped the situation by not even knowing why he had been called into hospital. Most patients may have queried the fact that they had only just arrived, so why were they now being sent home when nothing had been done. Finally the person who had left Tobias Tregonning's file along with the medical records of present patients must accept partial blame. If the file had been completed and sent off to the records department, the mistake would not have occurred.

So the rapid discharge of Thomas Tregonning came down to a genuine mistake, and senility or ignorance on behalf of Thomas himself. We had solved the problem and were sated with this little distraction to our otherwise monotonous day in hospital. Plus our sexy nurse wiggled even more over the next few days, just to show her appreciation.

Chapter Fourteen: Medication

There are very few people today that have not required some form of
medication at some point in their lives, from an anti-biotic to an over
the counter remedy for an upset stomach. There are those rare lucky
ones of course that may have escaped moments of pain, discomfort or
illness entirely, and I wish them well, honest . . . But most people
across the western world have at some time taken a tablet, potion,
concoction or remedy devised either by human science or by Mother
Nature. These days we tend to believe there is a pill for every ailment,
no matter how trivial or insignificant. We take travel pills, sea sickness
pills, altitude pills; weight loss pills, weight gain pills and vitamin pills.
We devour by the truck load such pills as paracetamol and
antihistamines almost as an integral part of our existence. In truth we
have become to depend on that little magical medicinal marvel of
modern science, known to us all as a pill or tablet.

   Using medication is an obviously important factor when one is
attempting to recover from illness or injury. Large numbers of people
require long term medication to combat diseases; others need
medication to relieve stress. Some just demand a form of medication
that releases them from the consequences of sexual activities. What
ever our reasons for using modern medication, the one indisputable fact
is that we now rely heavily on medical science, not just to keep us fit
and healthy or improve our sexual abilities, and there is even a pill for
that! It is also an indisputable fact that huge capacities of medication
used in hospitals, without medication a hospital would be little more
than a hotel. Medicine in all its shapes, forms, colours and uses fill
hospitals from floor to roof, administered by doctors who no longer

appear to wear white coats, and nurses who seem to get younger each time I require their services (*medical services I stress!*).

But it is not only in hospitals that the availability of medicine is found, most people now have ready access to drugs and treatments via a General Practioner or GP, Medical Doctor or MD or even a Witch doctor or Shaman if you like though one can never tell if one of their potions will cure you or turn you into a frog! A multitude of medication is available for almost all ailments in today's world, sometimes free, often expensive, but available all the same. And perhaps it is this ready availability that has confuses the poor patient, the accessibility to a million types of treatment. Or perhaps it is the long names, the unpronounceable names, the unintelligible names given to medicines that confound and bewilder the average person.

For some completely unknown reason, most people can recite from memory the ingredients to a favourite recipe or a list of book titles penned by their favourite author or what films their favourite celebrity appears in. However most cannot name or identify what medications they take daily. This creates quite a problem in hospitals, dealing with thousands of sick or injured patients each and every year. Doctors need to discover which drugs a patient is taking before prescribing a new course of treatment or a reduction of a specific drug. I always feel some pity for the medical staff when trying to obtain a patient's list of medication, not an easy task itself, as the mere fact that the person is now a patient indicates that person is not well and may be confused, tired, in pain or even unconscious! Yep I regularly see doctors and assorted medical professionals trying to get a verbal response from a comatose patient. In truth they know they will not get an answer, but it is their job to shout questions at each and every patient, conscious or not.

It is similarly astounding how many patients naturally assume doctors are clairvoyant. Especially the older generation, brought up to have complete faith in authority, never questioning, never disbelieving and completely reliant on figures in authority to guide them through their mundane lives. Many older patients firmly believe every doctor will know instinctively what medication they are presently taking and why.

'Doctor will know,' is often their reply when questioned on their treatment, even though the doctor presently treating them has never laid eyes on them before in his life!

Faith in doctors and the medical establishment is extremely high in the more mature person, it is the younger, more informed generations that are inclined to question, to seek answers for themselves and have the benefit of a modern education and the World Wide Web. Even so, still many patients, young or old have no idea what their drugs are called, what they are for and what interactions or side effects there may be as a consequence of administering such medication. So spare a thought for the medical professional next time you hear someone identify their list of medication with a list of colours.

The most common reply given by patients to doctors when asked about the individual's medication is, 'I take a white pill four times a day.'

It appears most people simply do not realise how many white tablets there are available today, describing the colour of a medication is probably one of the most useless pieces of information uttered in the vastness of the medical universe! As a frequent flyer in the medical hostelry industry, I have encountered many occasions when attempts made to clarify a patient's course of treatment have lead to confusion and surprise.

It was around mid morning and once again I was sitting quietly beside my hospital bed, trying to decide on taking a nap, reading a book, watching some mindless television or making a speedy dash down the corridor towards freedom! Luckily at that very moment a distraction occurred in the shape of a new patient intake. The rattle and crash of a carelessly manoeuvred patient trolley burst into the ward, an elderly man lying prone on its surface, his knuckles white as he held tightly to the side rails as if he were on a death defying fair ground attraction. Upon reaching his designated bed, the elderly gent was quickly and efficiently transferred from the trolley onto the bed and made comfortable, an expression of relief on his face at being rescued from the terrifying trolley transport.

As it was mid morning and the ward doctors were now fully awake with bellies sloshing from numerous cups of coffee, a doctor soon appeared at the gent's bedside. The young doctor introduced himself to the new patient and began his initial examination. This completed, the doctor enquired about any medication the elderly gent was already taking.

'Dunno what pills I take doctor,' replied the patient.

'No idea at all?'

'Well I take a white one, a blue one, two small red ones and a yellow one.'

'Do you know what they are for? What were you given them for?'

'Dunno doc, my GP gave 'em to me. Tis his job to know, not mine. I dunno 'bout medicines and such.'

'How do you know what tablets to take, and when to take them if you don't know what they are?' probed the doctor.

'Doctor wouldn't give 'em to me if I wasn't supposed to take 'em, would he? If he gave 'em to me, then I must need 'em in the first place!'

'What? So you follow your doctors instructions, is that what you mean?'

'No. 'Tis easier than that. I just take 'em all together.'

'Don't you have any that should only be taken once or twice a day?'

'Dunno doctor, can't really be bothered with all that. Can't remember which is which anyway, so I taken 'em all together.'

'Well does your wife know what medication you take?'

'No I don't have a wife; I take me pills by meself.'

'Oh good grief,' exclaimed the doctor, 'No wonder you're in here!'

As it turned out, the new patient had brought all his medications into hospital with him, so it was soon established exactly what drugs he was supposed to take, and when. But this occurrence is sadly far from unusual. In the case of married gentlemen, it is very often the wife who administers their husbands' tablets, dishing them out daily with meals or the obligatory glass of lukewarm water. Women appear to be better at organising their personal medication, however when it comes to reciting the names, again many refer simply to the colour.

One example of drug unawareness came when an important looking gent was admitted onto our ward. As is the case so often, those who are mainly fit have little conception of how the other half live. By other half I mean those of us who count the local hospital as our second home. We recurrent male inpatients only distinguish the difference between being at home or in hospital by the amount of women ordering us around. At home it is the wife or sister or sometimes a daughter or three. In hospital there always appear to be whole teams of women issuing orders, so we learn to differentiate between home and hospital by the increase or decrease in instructions and demands from authoritarian female figures.

The important looking gentleman was sat upright in his still tidy bed reading the Times newspaper with his spectacles perched on the tip of his nose. He had been polite but adamant that he really did not want to engage in conversation with the other patients in the ward. He had not long been admitted and as yet we knew nothing about him, so when the doctor arrived for the initial examination we hoped to gain more information by eavesdropping on their conversation. As I have mentioned before, even small distractions are still worth chasing when faced with the total boredom of hospital life. Curiosity swiftly sinking into simply being nosy!

Peering disdainfully over the rims of his spectacles, the important gentleman followed each of the doctor's commands and crisply answered all of his questions, until the subject of medication arose. It soon transpired the patient had no idea what treatment he was receiving, and he had also failed to bring his medication into hospital with him. Rejecting the rebuff from the doctor, the gentleman quietly informed the doctor it was his job to ascertain what his present medical condition was, and what medication was required to treat the ailment.

Quick as a flash the doctor replied that he was only a doctor, not a mind reader or fortune teller. He then enforced his own authority by stating it was the patient's sole responsibility to give notice of present medication and without this knowledge, no further treatment could be prescribed. The doctor then left the ward without a further word. When the important gentleman realised he was not so important after all, the next ten minutes were spent in desperate phone attempts to instruct a family member that his medication was required with all due haste.

In the vast majority of cases, a wife, husband or partner will rigidly follow instructions and advice when administering medication to their spouse. Occasionally this is not the situation.

Jerry Floyd was a new patient to our ward, only having arrived that day. He seemed quite fit and active compared to the rest of us; he even began trying to chat up nurses on his first day. Although Jerry was obviously quite ill, he still appeared to have surplus energy as he moved restlessly about the ward. Standing over 6 feet tall, slim with silver hair and a sparkle in his eyes. Jerry was certainly a friendly bloke, joining in our conversations and informing us about his condition and why he was in hospital. It appeared Jerry, who was well into his seventies, had a heart discrepancy and no one understood the cause. He had seen many doctors about his condition but to no avail, finally it was decided to admit him into hospital for tests. Jerry was completely unfazed by all this attention, though we soon realised he was not quite so unaffected by the presence of young attractive nurses. A fact soon noticed by the nurses themselves.

Jerry calmly answered all the doctor's enquiries, how long had he had this condition? Did he still pee alright, any problems with his bowels, how was his appetite. All the familiar questions designed to rule out the usual complaints of a man his age. However as with many others, when questioned about his medication he admitted he had no idea. Jerry informed the doctor that his wife laid out all his tablets with his meals, making sure he took the right medication at the correct time of day and in the right order. Jerry himself simply threw the pills down his throat without a second thought. Jerry told the doctor his wife would be in to visit that afternoon, so any information about his medication could be sought from her then. The doctor agreed and said he would return during visiting hours.

As the day wore on, we all noticed Jerry had begun to slowly wind down, the sparkle in his eye began to dim, the nurses could once more enter the ward in safety and his up right stature sagged slightly. This fact cheered all the other patients, including me; no one likes to feel inferior to a man in his seventies! Finally just before the allotted visiting time, Jerry fell asleep slumped in his bedside chair. No longer did he give the impression of a mature athlete, no more did he pace restlessly about the ward, in truth Jerry had declined into a normal pensioner.

Visiting time arrived and at two o clock in walked Jerry's wife. And as one, all our jaws hit the floor. She was gorgeous! Although not young, she was still much younger than Jerry, late forties or early fifties we were not sure. What we were sure of was her stunning figure and good looking appearance. Not too much make up and nor was she dangling with expensive jewellery, she was just a natural beauty that made all our hearts race and bedclothes rise. Not a good situation for those with pacemakers or weak hearts, but the vacant grins and slobbering chins gave a clear indication that the risk would possibly be worth it.

Jerry's wife approached his bed and looked down on his still sleeping figure, a slight frown of annoyance creasing her otherwise perfect brow. Gently she prodded him awake before removing her coat and making herself comfortable on a chair while Jerry gathered his thoughts and composure.

'Hello love,' muttered Jerry with a tired smile.

'Hello back to you. How are you today?'

'I'm fine really, just a bit tired. I don't know why, it's the first time I've felt like this for months.'

'Never mind, at least you're in hospital so they can take care of you. Have you been taking *all* your medication?' asked Jerry's wife.

'No sorry love, the young doctor wants to know what drugs I take at home but I don't know. So he's popping in to have a word with you while you're here, if that's OK?'

As Jerry completed his sentence, in walked the doctor and headed straight for Jerry's bed. Even though he was only in his late twenties, his face reflected his surprise as he too looked in amazement at the stunning figure beside Jerry's bed. Then a look of doubt clouded his face, he obviously could not decide if the beauty sat so prim was a wife, daughter, mistress or none of the above. So he hedged his bet.

'Hello. I'm Doctor Miles, I will be looking after Mr Floyd during his stay. And you are . . .?'

'Hi, yes I'm Jill, Jerry's wife. Pleased to meet you,' she replied with a small grin, she completely understood the young doctor's confusion.

'Well it's very nice to meet you Jill. I don't know if Mr Floyd has already explained but I need to know what medication he's taking at present. Do you have any with you or can you remember what drugs he's taking?' enquired the doctor while almost succeeding in professionally averting his gaze from the shapely bosom positioned perfectly before him.

'Yes I think I can remember the important ones, but some I still find hard to pronounce so I'll bring in all his medication when I visit again tomorrow, if that will do?'

'Certainly. That's fine, but if you can tell me which ones you remember I'll have a better idea on how to organise his treatment.'

Jerry's wife then listed several tablets to the doctor, names, amounts and frequency of administration. The doctor wrote down all that she told him, expressed his satisfaction with the list before bidding them both good day and leaving the ward. Jerry and Jill then both settled down to the light, meaningless conversation practised by patients and their visitors the world over.

My own wife arrived soon after, so my attention was ripped from the beauty across the room as I focused fully on my wife, as failing to do so would have most certainly resulted in dire consequences! Those patients without visitors that afternoon continued to covertly stare, drool and wish for all their might.

The next morning arrived early as usual with the nurses rushing into our ward like a horde of demons, frantically emptying urine bottles, straightening beds and issuing medication to still semi comatose patients. Jerry awoke grudgingly, acknowledged the nurses, and swallowed his pills and promptly collapsed back to sleep. We still had an hour or so before breakfast so some patients like me also took the opportunity to return to the comfortable land of nod. The other more awake patients began the ritual file to the bathroom in an attempt to beat the after breakfast rush.

When the breakfast trolley finally rattled and crashed into the room, we all immediately prepared ourselves for the first entertainment of the day. Except Jerry, he really did not want to be awoken, and groaned and moaned between each mouthful of cold toast and marmalade. As the morning progressed we began to have serious concerns about Jerry. The up right man full of vigour and vitality had completely disappeared, even the nurses noticed the change in him. A stern looking female doctor was called and came in to check Jerry over but could find no signs of anything further amiss. Finally it was decided to wait until his wife arrived in the afternoon so all his medication could be checked, in case he was missing an important part of his treatment. However, to be safe the doctor ordered hourly observations and requested that she be notified of any further deterioration. Through the morning and mid day no improvement or decline showed in Jerry's demeanour so a waiting game ensued. Jerry did not appear to be declining in health as such, he had simply begun to act as any normal seventy year old would be expected to, it was the observation that he was now a different person to the one that bounced into the ward yesterday that caused concern.

At last the hour for visiting arrived and both staff and doctor eagerly awaited the arrival of Jerry's wife. As a matter of interest, so did the majority of us patients, but for an entirely different reason. Some visitors had already arrived and made themselves comfortable or at least as comfortable as possible on the hard, cold plastic chairs provided for use by non patients. Soon the click, click of high heels coming along the corridor foretold the arrival of Jerry's stunning spouse. A chain reaction occurred as all the still red blooded male patients began surreptitiously straightening bed clothes, hiding porn magazines, urine bottles, combing hair and ensuring the correct positioning of pyjamas, false teeth and wigs.

Jerry's wife entered the room with a waft of perfume and a smile. Greeting Jerry she sat down beside his bed, giving him a delicate kiss on his forehead as she moved down onto the chair. Jerry did not appear quite so tired at this time and smiled with obvious pleasure at her arrival.

'So how are you today love?' asked Jill.

'Not so bad love, still a bit tired and not quite myself, but nothing to worry about. Before I forget, did you bring in all my pills?'

'Yes love, I'll sort them out for you in a moment. Do those other patients always stare at you? It's weird!'

'Ah ha, don't bother about them, it's you they're staring at and I don't blame them, you look gorgeous today,' laughed Jerry as all we fellow patients quickly looked away, embarrassed at being caught out.

To add to our discomfort, Jill turned and smiled brightly at each of us in turn, teasing as only an attractive woman can. One by one we all smiled back at her before becoming quickly engrossed in a book, magazine or the bedside television and even our own visitors in an attempt to hide our red faces.

Jerry and his wife Jill lapsed into conversation about family and friends at home for a few minutes before Jerry suggested they check the medication she had brought from home before calling the doctor. Jill swung her ample handbag onto the bed and began rustling inside it. One by one packets and bottles of tablets were produced then laid out on the bed. While this was happening, the doctor who had requested the medication saw them both and changed his direction towards Jerry and Jill.

'I see you've brought in Mr Floyd's medication, thank you. Is this everything?' asked the doctor.

'Yes,' replied Jill, quickly.

'That's fine, I'll just note what's here and adjust your drug chart accordingly. There doesn't appear to be anything of significance here so you haven't missed out on anything important. OK, that's it all done. Now before I go, one last check nothing has been forgotten, can you think of any medication not taken regularly, or left in the car?

Anything like that?' enquired the doctor as he completed copying down
the list of medication names and doses.

'No nothing,' replied Jill before her husband could speak.

'Hang on love,' interjected Jerry, 'What about that small white
one? I'm sure I saw them in your bag a moment ago.'

'What small white one is that Mrs Floyd?' asked the doctor.

'Oh that's nothing, just an aspirin because Jerry gets a
headache occasionally, that's all,' replied Jill as she reached out and
closed her bag.

'I think you should show the doctor love, it could be
important.'

'No it's OK, it's nothing.'

'Please love? What's the harm?'

'Oh fine!' snapped Jill while reaching for her bag and digging
in it. Finally her hand found a small brown bottle with six white tablets
in it. Grudgingly she passed the bottle to the doctor.

'See? It's only aspirin,' muttered Jill.

The doctor peered into the bottle then emptied one of the
tablets out into his hand. He peered at the small white tablet in an
attempt to recognise its properties few a few moments, turning the tablet
around in his hand.

'Excuse me a moment,' he said as he quickly left the room, a
deep frown on his face.

'Wonder what's wrong with him?' said Jerry to his concerned
looking wife.

'I don't know,' she replied hesitantly, 'Perhaps he's just
checking what dosage the aspirin is.'

Minutes later the doctor returned. Holding out the tablet in his
hand, he looked accusingly at Jill.

'Do you know what this is?' he asked her quietly.

'Yes.'

'Where did you get it?'

Caught unaware but fully understanding the doctor's accusing stare, Jill replied, 'I'd rather not say.'

'OK then, why have you been giving your husband this drug?'

'Well he just keeps falling asleep and has no energy for anything, and I do mean anything! I thought it might help perk him up, in more ways than one, if you get my meaning?'

'Oh yes, I do. However if you were concerned about your husbands state of health, you could have checked with his doctor first.'

'Hey, hang on here!' exclaimed Jerry, 'What's going on? Why all the fuss over a simple aspirin?'

'It's not aspirin is it Mrs Floyd?' enquired the doctor, quietly.

'No.'

'In fact Mr Floyd, this tablet your wife has been giving you is an amphetamine!'

'What?'

'A narcotic, a street drug. Speed as it is often called.'

'Oh crap,' sighed Jerry.

'Well I only wanted him to get the most out of life, especially as he's getting on a bit in years now. I didn't want to embarrass him by saying anything so I managed to acquire these to help him out. I didn't mean any harm; I just want him to be the man I married. I'm sorry Jerry,' Jill finished with a small sob.

Taking pity on the couple, the doctor relented. Mr and Mrs Floyd were obviously distressed, Jill because of what she had been administering to her unwitting husband, and Jerry in total confusion.

The doctor then explained to Jerry that this form of amphetamine was a strong *upper* narcotic, or stimulant, a substance that used to be known as '*Speed*'. Reassuring Jerry that the dosage he had been given was not too harmful, the doctor then turned to Jill and asked for a list of symptoms that lead her to sneaking a narcotic into Jerry's daily treatment list.

Jill described how Jerry kept constantly falling asleep or dozing off, no matter what he was doing at the time. Jill had managed to persuade Jerry to stop driving for his own safety and that of others. But in matters relating to the bedroom for instance, Jerry's habit of dozing off had become quite frustrating. Jill mentioned a few more symptoms while watching both the doctor's and Jerry's eye brows climb further and further up their foreheads. At last the doctor could take no more and began to chuckle, much to Jerry's annoyance, he was imaging his wife had been trying to poison him!

'The problem you're describing sounds very much like Narcolepsy. It's quite common and can be safely treated, strangely enough with a medication very similar to what you've already been giving your husband. It's called Dexamphetamine and we can prescribe it here. However I would suggest we run tests on your husband to make certain of this prognosis and we should be able to come up with a treatment that is not just safer, but will only cost you the price of a prescription, slightly less than what you paid for these I would assume?'

'Er . . yes, thank you doctor,' whispered Jill in embarrassment and guilt.

'I can also prescribe some medication to er . . enhance his performance if you feel it's necessary?' questioned the doctor quietly.

'No thank you. All is fine in that area. When he manages to stay awake at least,' muttered Jill in a whispered response.

So the moral of this story is, if you have a younger and very attractive wife, make sure you are always up to performing your marital obligations. And always ensure you learn about, and administer your medications yourself!

However good looks and a younger partner are not solely to blame for some odd occurrences when a husband, wife, boyfriend, toy boy, sugar daddy or mistress is in charge of their partner or spouse's medication. Age is often no barrier either.

I was lying peacefully in my hospital bed, barely awake and desperately trying to remember what delights I had ordered from the hospital lunch menu, when chaos erupted behind the screens of the bed opposite mine. I knew a very old gent had arrived and been placed in that bed some time earlier that same morning. As yet I had no idea as to his condition, but from the state of him when he came in, it was not good. A small frail looking gent, lying still and drawn on his bed, with his eyes closed. A similarly small but rotund elderly woman sat perched nervously on the little plastic chair beside his bed, holding his pale hand and whispering comforts to his unresponsive ear.

Doctors had arrived quickly and the screens were pulled round the bed as they began their examination. Although hidden from view, their voices and that of the elderly woman could be clearly heard around the room. The conversation and questions flowed normally as the doctors attempted to ascertain the small gents condition, and I quickly began to lose interest in eves dropping as sleep was gently covering me with its blanket.

Suddenly I was rudely awoken by the rise in volume as the conversation grew heated and increased in volume behind the screen opposite me. The doctors were trying to explain to the woman sat there that her husband's condition was due to exhaustion. It had quickly come to light that she had been regularly slipping a very well known sexual stimulant in his course of medication. Her reason she stated, was that she did not feel old and still enjoyed certain activities unlike her husband who now needed some *assistance*!

But by far the biggest misuse of medication is the failure to follow or understand instructions. I have witnessed many cases in and out of hospital of people being prescribed new medication, but because the doctor did not specifically tell them to stop their old medication, they continued to take both at once. Obviously this will cause serious medical issues, but who's to blame? The doctor for assuming that in the twenty first century, patients will have the intelligence to realise they should discontinue taking the old medication, or the patient for being so stupid.

So when taking medication for any form of ailment, illness, disease or injury, it will always benefit the patient to learn and understand what it is they are taking, and why. Try not to blindly rely on doctors knowing one's entire medical history, and be very careful when accepting medication from over sexed or vain spouses! And also pay strict attention to your life insurance policies, just in case.

Chapter Fifteen: Strange Behaviour.

Many people have witnessed strange or odd behaviour from fellow
patients in hospital, with some this behaviour is intentional while with
others it is not. When a person is very ill the mind plays tricks and
seems to take over memories, desires or sad events that can then be
replayed over and over again in the patient's head, often leading to them
acting out scenes from the past. The scenes while perfectly rational to
the sick person are totally baffling and occasionally quite humorous to
those looking on. Many, many people go through this stage when very
ill though few remember the events once they have recovered. It is with
noted with pleasure that virtually all those who have gone through this
stage eventually recover totally and return to their homes and families.
There is a phrase or saying in some hospitals now, the noisy ones will
eventually recover, it's the quiet ones who need our prayers. Hence this
telling of the antics, odd behaviour and events that have been witnessed
over the years is not derogatory to those people concerned; it is simply a
narration of their road to recovery and return to good health. As an
example and maybe an explanation I will begin with a story about one
of my own.

I had been ill for some time; the manner of my illness is not
important, save to say it was fast beginning to annoy me. I was very
young, early teens I think and the prospect of being trapped in hospital
was not my idea of fun. I was in a small room with only two or three
other patients, in what was the teenage section of a children's ward.
This section was partitioned off from the main ward to offer some
privacy and quiet to we older children who no longer regarded ourselves
as kids, even though we obviously were. As with all teenagers, the
desire to *grow up* was very strong in me. Strange considering that now

I am fully grown I am still getting into trouble as I refuse to be a serious old fuddy duddy or a grumpy old fart and often get accused of being childish!

It was an old hospital and included many features not seen in today's modern box designed medical constructions. It also meant it did not have many of the modern features we take for granted in our super bug infested venues of kill or cure medicinal practice. Things like a reliable central heating system, draft proof windows or individual bedside lamps. I mention these three items because they each play a part in this story, as will become clear, eventually.

The ward was quite small, room only for the four beds and included some assorted ancient medical equipment like thumb screws, racks and leeches. The ceilings were high and the one sole window was of the wooden sash variety, narrow and tall and over looked a section of the city and its bright lights in the valley below. Pale red night lights in the shape of long narrow rectangles were situated on the wall just above the floor, designed to illuminate a nurse's way in the darkness. These lights were destined to become a thing of the past when individual bedside lamps came into being, thankfully removing the need to switch on the bright ceiling lights when ever a patient needed attention. There is nothing worse than being ill in hospital, having difficulty sleeping and as soon as one nods off, someone turns on those damn lights, jerking you awake seconds before blinding you.

I could not distinguish many of the room's features as I was sealed tightly into an old fashioned oxygen tent, the type that used to cover an entire bed like a plastic bubble. Luckily this is yet another old medical device that is seldom seen or used in modern medicine. It was uncomfortably hot much of the time, isolated from the surrounding world, including visitors, fellow patients luckily; and any form of normal human interaction. Sadly it excluded a lovely young female school pre-leaver who was volunteering at the hospital at that time on a work experience programme. The oxygen tent did have slits placed at strategic positions along the sides, with zip fasteners which allowed arms to be inserted into the tent so medication and care plus the odd meal or drink could be administered, without me escaping the bubble. It also allowed an angel to insert a soft hand into my plastic world.

The young school girl spent hours beside my plastic cocoon trying to ease my pain and suffering with her huge heart and truly caring spirit. Sitting beside my bed with one arm through an unzipped slit, she comforted me by gently rubbing my back while maintaining a dialog of soothing but one sided conversation, an action that meant more to me at that time than all the medication in the world! Unfortunately I was simply too ill to note at the time that I was being cared for by an angel. A teenage girl, blond, very shapely developed and just the sort of medicine a puberty empowered male teenager would normally dream of, in his lonely bedroom with one hand active beneath the bedclothes. Her visits were far too brief regrettably and all too soon I was alone once more in my own plastic hell.

Looking at the world through a plastic bubble and with eyes tired from fighting ill health is difficult to say the least! Even when fully awake my mind had trouble interpreting the strange images that drifted into my vision from within my giant supermarket plastic shopping bag. It was this distorted view of the world that initiated my own odd behaviour and caused frequent good humoured jibs for my remaining time in that hospital.

It was a foul night, rain lashed against the window opposite me, hiding the city lights in its ferocity as it poured down each small individual window pane. The room was quiet other than the wind whistling through the gaps in the old window, creating the effect of a blizzard howling outside. No sounds of breathing or movement came from the other young patients sharing the ward and I began to dream I was alone. It was quite late, moving towards the very early hours of the morning and no one stirred, not even the idle chatter from nurses filtered through to my troubled mind. I had been drifting in and out of sleep throughout the night but this time when I awoke, things had changed. My world was strange, new and unfamiliar, yet I felt I had existed there for millennia as a scene swam before my eyes that I could not immediately comprehend. The ward had gone. Nor did I have any recollection of ever being on that ward. Instead I was looking out through sick eyes at the interior of a log cabin. Being a particularly insensitive sort of teenager, I first wondered what the hell I was watching on telly. It didn't occur to me that in those dark and distant days long ago, television shut down around midnight, leaving only a slowly diminishing white dot to hold the attention of the most avid viewer. When I realised I was not peering at a television, the hospital had not yet caught up with modern entertainment technology anyway, the next question that sprang into my mind was, what was I doing in a log cabin? I had never been in one before in my life!

As I looked around this strange room, filled with a dying log fire, snow piling up on the outside window frame, a roughly built table and two chairs to one side and a heap of fire wood on the other, my mind began to fill in the details from the depths of my imagination. The images my mind decided to supply could best be described as a practical joke. I was now playing tricks on myself. Very strange!

I could no longer see my fellow patients, they did not exist. The observation window that allowed staff to check our ward from the main children's ward next door had disappeared. The ceiling had lowered and consisted of wooden planks secured on top of huge wood beams. Each wall was constructed of logs, laying one on top of the other and filled with some kind of mud or other natural sealant to stop drafts, snakes, insects and peeping toms gaining access to the room. The fire glowed with dying ashes, its weak red light casting small shadows and faintly picking out the rug covered floor around my bed. My world had become cosy and peaceful, I had no idea what I was doing there and I did not care. Aliens, Dr Who, CIA, MI6, even Jehovah Witnesses or some other figment of my imagination could have kidnapped me, and carried me off to this rustic cabin in the middle of nowhere and I did not care. I was content, not sick, not hungry, no pain nor any real sense of reality, my perfect world.

Suddenly a figure entered my peaceful cabin, a dark shape unrecognised. The figure drifted silently towards me before bending carefully over my resting form, still I did not care. Apparently satisfied with what it had seen, the figure wafted round the room stopping occasionally to inspect the table and chairs, the fire wood heap and the window. It was then I remembered the dying embers of the fire.

'Hey,' I shouted weakly, 'Stick some more wood on the fire will you? It's nearly out.'

I received no reply; the figure simply moved to my bed again and once more peered at me.

'Please, put some wood on the fire, it's about to go out,' I asked again.

'It's OK, no need to worry,' said a quiet voice that floated in the air.

'Yes there bloody well is!' I insisted, 'The damn fire is dying and it's bloody cold outside. Stick some wood on the fire. Please!'

'Hush. Go back to sleep.'

'How the hell can I sleep when the bloody fire is dying? I'll bloody freeze!'

'Hush, you'll disturb the others. Go to sleep,' replied the airborne voice.

This disembodied voice was beginning to pee me right off! Why the hell wouldn't they listen? Maybe it's a ghost I thought, no good asking a ghost to put wood on the fire, they can not touch anything. And why did it keep telling me to go to sleep? And what was the damn thing doing in my quiet log cabin anyway?

As most teenagers I was very quick to lose my temper, frustration aided by puberty and the fact that I had no idea where I was nor who or what the dark figure was, fired my dim brain into action. I leapt extremely slowly from my bed, straight into an invisible barrier which slapped me back again. I felt strangely weak but my teenage temper goaded me into sorting this stupid, soft spoken figure out. Up again I sprang; eventually, once again I was forced back onto my bed by the unseen force, and all the while the dark figure simply stood and watched me.

'I'll brain the bugger,' I thought, 'just let me get hold of it.' These and other such pleasant thoughts whirled through my mind as I struggled to free myself from this invisible envelope.

'Put some bloody wood on the fire before I stick your head in it!' I shouted again, 'It's not difficult, just put wood on the fire. Now!'

On and on I raged, demanding the dying fire should be feed, cursing the dark figure that stood silently over me throughout the remaining night hours. Many times I attempted to leap from my bed and beat the living daylights out of the dark apparition, but something kept me at bay, something I could not see. Finally as dawn approached I gave up my battle and eased into an uncomfortable sleep once more, not caring that the dark figure still silently watched me.

The daylight hours came and went with me noting only small snippets of time passing as I dozed, slept and struggled with my illness. Night dropped and again lifted its curtain before I awoke fully. Feeling better, my mind was sharper and details of where I was and why I was here filtered back into my brain. This took some time, everyone knows how difficult it is to wake a teenager and I was no different.

'Would you like a cup of tea?' a voice said from a distorted face floating outside my bubble and finishing the complicated business of waking up.

I opened my eyes fully to the mid morning glare of the world, scratched those parts that always require scratching in the morning before replying that I would like a cup of tea.

'Ahh! Hello, glad to see you're back with us. How are you feeling?' asked the nurse in my limited field of vision.

I replied that I was feeling fine and when could I go home? The nurse laughed and went on her way, obviously satisfied with my recovery and therefore required no more attention for the time being. It was true, I felt I had reached a turning point and was eager to be squeezed out of my bubble and back into the real world. I knew I had been ill, but that was in the past, today I was already fed up with hospital and wanted release. Later that same day I did get released from the oxygen tent and for the first time I fully and coherently took note of my fellow patients and my surroundings. I shared the room with three other lads, all around my age and all appeared slightly uncertain about enjoining a conversation with me. Fine I thought; if you want to be like that then so be it. Again being a teenager, I put this thought into words with a sneer as I informed the other patients they could go forth and multiply!

Alas I was wrong. Almost immediately one of the bigger lads climbed from his bed and headed for me. Oh crap! I thought, I didn't realise he was allowed out of bed. I need not have worried, he had not come to splatter my few brains against the wall, but instead he gently sat at the foot of my bed and quietly asked how I was feeling?

'I'm fine,' I mumbled in reply.

'That's good. You were in some state, dunno what's wrong with you but you sure got everyone's attention for a while.'

'Why? What did I do? I didn't do anything.'

'You did! You kept us all awake with your shouting the night before last. What the heck were you talking about anyway? There ain't no fire in here. Except the one we're gonna light under your bed if you go shouting like that again when we want to sleep,' ended the big boy with a snarl.

'No I bloody didn't!'

'Yes you bloody did!' he snarled again.

The row continued with the other two boys joining in. I was getting increasingly annoyed, what the hell were they talking about? I did not shout anything about a fire. Finally the nurse returned to see what the raucous was about, just in time actually because I was ready to leap from my bed and attack the boy, no matter how much bigger he was. Shooing the big boy back to his bed, the nurse explained that I had been shouting about a fire but that was because I had been very ill. The soothing voice of the nurse triggered my still confused memories and I began to recall the strange dream I had about the log cabin. My defences breeched, I decline to argue further, instead I lapsed into a typical teenage sulk for an hour or so, but as with all childhood disagreements, we all forgot the episode and got on with terrorising the hospital as only young teenagers can.

So that is my story, I hope it would help explain the actions of those to follow. When very ill we are all liable to act in peculiar ways. Not because we are mentally unbalanced but because our bodies are fighting the illness or injury and just like a computer, our minds scan files of all memories in an attempt to find an answer to our predicament. It is our defence mechanism, our survival traits coming to the fore. It is both our bodies and our minds healing themselves.

That is one of my personal stories, I have many more but now it is time to move on to stories of strange behaviour exhibited by others as seen from my hospital bed.

Again as an adult, I found myself once again in an establishment of alleged medical repute. It was a quiet night on the ward; most of the patients were sleeping or readying themselves for sleep when it happened. A patient in the bed immediately opposite mine suddenly leapt from his bed covers with eye wide and mouth open in a silent scream. Quickly he stood up on his bed and peered up at the wall behind him. High up on that wall a small window allowed a cheerful, when not raining, view of the sky, reminding us that there was a life on the outside to return to. The patient was scrabbling towards this window and upon reaching it; he opened it and proceeded to attempt his escape. The poor patient completely failed to understand in his fuddled state, that he could never fit his body through such a small opening. Much like the camel and the rich man trying to squeeze through the eye of a needle, this chap had absolutely no chance of success, but it didn't stop him trying.

'The ship is on fire! Everyone out! Get of the ship before we burn!' he suddenly began shouting.

Immediately all the other patients on the ward began paying full attention to the events unfolding before us. A patient climbing onto his bed to open a window caused little interest, even when he attempted to climb out, but a tall, thin patient wearing only brief underpants leaping up and down on his bed screaming '*Fire*' did get our notice!

On and on he screamed his eyes wide as he implored us all to evacuate the burning ship. Nothing we said calmed him down, he was totally absorbed in his frantic delusion and desperate to save all our lives. Frantically our fingers jabbed at the nurse call bell but night staff number less than day staff and they were obviously already very busy, so none answered our calls immediately. Finally, in the far corner bed, a patient named Flynn quietly but forcefully called to the hysterical patient.

'What deck?'

'The third deck, the galley is on fire!' was the response.

'Fire team are on the way. Stay calm and give directions when they arrive,' ordered Flynn.

'Yes Sir!'

At this command the jumping patient ceased his attempts to escape through what he obviously took for a porthole and sat back onto his bed. Just like buses, you wait ages for one and finally several turn up together, so it was as numerous nurses and a doctor rushed in, casting worried glances around the ward, confused by the unusual number of illuminated nurse call buttons brightening the ward with their orange glow. Demands for information came swift and sure from the night duty doctor who appeared to realise this was no joke.

As the panicked patient was now sitting quietly on the side of his bed, Flynn offered an update on the recent events and asked the doctor to approach the man and tell him the fire team were present and that the situation was under control. Of course the doctor refused at first, not being able to comprehend what was asked of him. But a stern command by Flynn accompanied by demands from fellow patients ensured the doctor eventually did as requested.

'Fire team on station,' announced the doctor following a prompt from Flynn, 'Please remain where you are for assessment by the medical team.'

'Yes Sir!' replied the still confused patient as he allowed the doctor to approach him and begin his examination.

The situation was now under control and the hospital staff administered to the now quiet but possibly still delirious patient with a small tranquiliser injection into his arm. When all was silent, Flynn was asked for an explanation which he grudgingly gave. It transpired that Flynn himself was an ex naval officer and immediately recognised the poor patient was reliving a frightening event from his career. Flynn explained he too had been caught in a fire on board ship and hence understood just how terrifying the situation could be. By shouting an order requesting further information, the patient had responded automatically, slipping back into his training and deferring to authority. What Flynn had recognised we other patients learned fully some time later. The panicked patient was indeed a sailor and had once been almost trapped in a galley fire. Flynn's prompt action had saved the day, saved our hospital *ship* from burning, and calmed a feverish mind in a very poorly sailor.

Not so humorous a story, but one I thought to include as an insight into why many very sick people act so strangely when in a hospital. The action taken by Flynn had instant results and saved the patient from bucket loads of calming medication, possible psychiatric treatment and a total lack of understanding by those trying to help him. There was no way the medical staff could have known the sailor would hysterically act out his worst nightmare in the peace and safety of a hospital ward without Flynn's intervention.

The sailor eventually made a full recovery with no more nightmares or delusions.

Then there was the Door Man. Not a professional security person or Bouncer as they used to be known, but an old, wizened and tiny man with a desperate desire to escape and be somewhere else.

All day and every day, this old gent would try every door on the ward, his constant mobility caused him to sweat and puff as he moved from door to door without rest. What type of door did not matter, cupboards, fire exits, laundry rooms, staff rooms and toilet doors, all received his attention throughout the day. All the patients quickly learned to lock toilet doors when occupied; it can be embarrassing to have the toilet door flung wide while one is straining at ones business! The nurses tried constantly to stop his antics and caringly lead him back to his bed each time, only for him to jump swiftly back on his feet and resume his quest. He was obstinate, trying each and every door within the department over and over again. When questioned why he was trying to get out of the ward, he would give a look, a look that suggested it was obvious and that the questioner was either stupid or ignorant.

'I must meet my wife,' was the routine reply, 'I can't stay here!'

Off he would go again, doors that would open were pushed wide as he peered into what ever room or cupboard the door belonged to. If the door was locked and refused to open, a period of pushing, kicking and thumping followed as he vainly attempted to bash the door down until a member of staff located the ancient vandal and again returned him to his bed.

Unfortunately for me, my bed was situated near a locked double door which lead to another room that was mainly used for teaching but could also be adapted as an over flow ward if the need arose, hence the adjoining doors. Hundreds of times during both day and night I would hear the slap of slippered feet heading towards this door. Then the kicking, rattling of handles and thumping on the wooden door would shatter the silence before he moved on to examine the next one.

I will admit the old gent was no wimp, even though he was much older than me, smaller and weaker, my words of discouragement bothered him not a jot. If I asked politely or even impolitely to leave the damn door alone and go away, he would just snarl at me and inform me it was none of my business! Other patients also tried to dissuade him from attacking every door in sight non stop throughout the day and into the night, but to no avail. The medical staff administered a mild sedative but it was no use, it did not even slow him down. Off he would go again; opening or trying to open every door he came across.

After a while we all became accustomed to his antics and tried hard to ignore him, after all he was not actually causing anyone any harm, and it appeared to keep him busy and active if nothing else. The only times he did cause concern was when he discovered the door leading into the women's section of the ward. A whole new ward to explore for doors! This of course was not acceptable and he was quickly ushered back to his own bay and bed. But the draw of the new unexplored ward was too much of a temptation and off he would set again. No one feared him or was unduly concerned about his behaviour; he was a tiny old man and could not harm a fly. But it was still very disconcerting for the lady patients when a frantic little man appeared at their bedside, opening locker doors, cupboard doors and any other door that resembled an escape route. Most patients and staff understood it was his medication and illness causing him to act that way, so most some became tolerant and stood aside to let him continue his endless search, providing he avoided the women's ward, which he did not and was constantly being lead away.

Finally the old gent was considered recovered enough to be transferred to another ward more suitable to his age and condition. We all sighed with relief and looked forward to an uninterrupted night's sleep, without the constant rattling of door handle, thumping or kicking going on into the wee hours of the night.

Strangely none of us could answer or understand why the only door in the whole ward he did not try to open, was the exit itself! Perhaps it was because this double door had windows and all he would be able to see was the blank wall opposite. It obviously never occurred to him that the outside corridor was at right angles to the ward, all he needed to do was push open the door and turn right, this would have taken him out of the ward and onto the main exit corridor.

It became know a few days after the doorman had been moved to a more suitable ward that he was in fact a widower, his wife having died years ago. It seems that even long after her demise, the poor old man was still attempting to follow some request or instruction she had made in the past. He was still a totally devoted, or subjugated, husband! Eventually his health improved and his antics ceased, he was discharged back to his friends in a nursing home where he had lived for the last decade or so.

Next there was the bed hopper. A large, round bellied middle aged man who continually found his way into other patient's beds, occupied or not! This was quite disconcerting to we fellow patients, most of us did not appreciate the prospect of discovering an over weight gentleman lifting our sheets in order to gain entrance to our own snug hospital bed. I say most of us because I am not too sure about at least one patient who did not seem to mind at all!

Luckily it soon became apparent that the middle aged gentleman did not *bat for the other side* nor was he deliberately forcing his attentions on any of us. He simply had an extremely poor memory. We soon discovered that due to his medication, he could no longer orientate his surroundings. Rising out from his own bed to visit the toilet or stretch his legs, he would wonder out of the ward where a kindly nurse or medical assistant would guide him to his intended destination. However when he came back into the ward, he would head for any of the beds that appealed as he had already forgotten which one was actually his. The fact that the sought after bed was already occupied still did not deter him, and he would strive to enter that bed.

Once the facts behind his behaviour were known, we all made a concerted effort to direct him to his own bed space as soon as he re-entered the room. The only trouble occurred at night, if he had to relieve himself when the rest of us were sleeping, some one was in for a rude awakening!

Imagine swollen testicles! One patient had the extreme misfortune to suffer an unusual side effect from the medication he was receiving. His testicles grew enlarged, very enlarged!

The patient was a huge man, pleasant and friendly, keeping us all entertained with his humorous regalia about his work and odd memories. The reason for his hospital stay was common knowledge, he had cheerfully informed us all as to why, when, where and what. But the issue that was causing him the greatest discomfort was the fact that he had reacted to some of his treatment, a side effect that resulted in water being retained and sinking into his testicles.

Every time an unsuspecting doctor or nurse passed his bed, they were accosted and given a full frontal view of the offending body parts, accompanied a plea for help.

'My balls hurt! They're too bloody swollen! Can you give me something for them please?'

This uninhibited behaviour was bad enough for we other patients, as this large fellow continually lifted his hospital gown without any thoughts to dignity or modesty. Full frontal views were common, worse at meal times and visitors often had the shock of their lives!

The medical staff understood the chap's pain and discomfort, however he needed a specific medication at that time and once the medication was finished, the swelling would go down. The poor chap was informed of this fact daily, but his obvious fear of spending the rest of his life with two cricket ball sized appendages hanging low between his legs was too much for his mind to endure. Until then, everyone avoided going anywhere near his bed, and if this manoeuvre could not be accomplished, all made sure they averted their gaze. Regrettably for me, my bed was right opposite to his, in a direct visual line, almost unavoidable. Every time the gown came up, or the cricket balls flopped, I had to either avert my sensitive gaze, or run screaming from the room!

Now everyone knows that some people walk in their sleep and some people talk in their sleep, a fact that has landed many a husband in deep trouble when the morning comes with a very irate wife demanding to know who Mandy or Sharon or Tracy was! The poor husband, sleep still encrusting his eyes has to frantically form an excuse for a dream he cannot remember!

Sleep talkers are rarely a nuisance, but this is not always the case. One time while an inpatient yet again, I had the misfortune to share a ward with two sleep talkers. This fact alone did not bother me too much, until they began holding a conversation with each other in their sleep!

'Oy! Who are you?' shouted the first,

'Dunno, what you doing 'ere?' relied the second.

'Where's me van?' asked the first.

'I gotta get back to my shop,' stated the second sleep talker.

'Where's John? He's s'posed to be 'ere,' muttered the first.

'Is he in me shop?' answered the second.

This strange conversation continued for thirty minutes or more before a nurse came into the ward and attempted to quieten the two talkers. A small success was won, both talkers ceased their mutterings, but not for long.

'Oy! Who are you?' called the first sleep talker again.

'Steve!' was the short reply.

'Who? What you doing in me van?'

'Tis my shop. That you John?' grunted the second talker, still fast asleep.

Though neither patient was consciously speaking to the other, the mutterings and calls from each sleeping patient appeared to hold the lines of a conversation, disjointed in places but a conversation all the same.

Once again the nurse entered the ward and this time she ensured both participants were awake before scolding them to be quiet. Alas it was not to be, the two avid talkers continued their broken conversation sporadically throughout the night. Being familiar with the antics of patients during the night time hours, I buried my head under my pillow and tried to sleep. I had no real hope of achieving much rest as this was my first night back in hospital and I often hardly sleep on my initial night. Sometimes it is due to illness or discomfort, sometimes it is the medication that combats sleep, sometimes it is the pure shock at finding myself wrenched from my comfortable and loving home and imprisoned in a small room full of strange men doing what strange men do during the night!

'That's me wife. What you doing with Nancy? Yer bugger!' growled the first suddenly into the darkness.

'Who you calling a bugger? Tis my wife, not yours!' shouted the second in reply.

'Here, let go me Nancy or I'll belt ya!' screamed the first.

'I'll bloody have you if you don't bugger off!'

'Come on then, let's be 'aving you. I'll teach you to mess 'round with my missus!'

'No, I'll teach you!'

With that, both talkers began thrashing around in their beds, both still deeply asleep and both fighting for the honour of their respective wives. Suddenly the unconscious battle came to an end, as one of the antagonists dream induced struggles resulted in him falling out of bed with a crash, taking a bedside table with him. The other patients continued to writhe about in his bed before becoming still a moment later.

'What's going on?' demanded one of the two nurses that had hurried into our ward at the sound of the commotion.

'Huh?' answered the patient now sat in an untidy heap on the floor beside his bed.

'What are you doing down there? You should be in bed,' said one of the nurses stating the obvious while bending to help the patient onto his feet. The other nurse stood close by, ready in case the patient fell again.

'Dunno, think I was having a bad dream. Some bloke was trying to steal away me missus so I belted him,' answered the patient as he struggled to his feet.

The second of the two sleep talkers was still sound asleep, though he was not talking now. After the nurses straightened his bed and helped the now wide awake patient back into his bed, peace settled on the ward like an assuring blanket, allowing all of us to maintain a reasonable level of unconsciousness for the remainder of the night.

In the morning the two talkers showed no inkling of the night's events, both grunted a morning greeting to the other patients and devoured their breakfast in silence. But one question held strong in my mind and soon the urge to discover the answer drove me to speak.

'Morning all,' I said to no one in particular, 'as a matter of interest, what's your wives called?'

'Nancy,' was the reply in unison from the two night sleepers. Strange!

Chapter Sixteen: Politically correct Henry.

One particular patient provided huge amounts of entertainment to his fellow patients and ward staff throughout his stay in hospital. His rustic humour and total lack of embarrassment proved a constant source of amusement and his broad, thick country accent added to the situation.

He was a stocky man in his late sixties, with thinning fair hair, now fading to gray, a strong square face and ready smile. A barrel chest, wide shoulders and muscular arms portrayed a life of hard demanding work; Henry was a man to be reckoned with. He was a farmer by trade and successfully farmed both livestock and crops in a period where most farmers were struggling to make a decent living.

Henry had not been in hospital before so had no idea of, nor concerns over the usual etiquette of a hospital. Before he gave respect it had to be earned, the title of doctor or consultant meant nothing to him. He spoke as he saw fit and when he felt something needed saying, he said it. From calling one young doctor a '*bloody nuisance*', to describing a physiotherapist as a '*paid sadist*' and telling the nurses in no uncertain terms that they were not going to give him an all over bed bath! Henry considered a bed bath by very young nurses to be against his idea of decency, he would wait for his wife to visit and she would administer his ablutions. Henry was extremely old fashioned in many of his beliefs and being manhandled by young women was totally out of order in his opinion. He was not going to embarrass himself by reacting to the administrations of young girls messing with his private parts! Henry of course did not realise the nurses would not be exploring his privates, these days the cleaning flannel or sponge is handed to the patient so they themselves can administer to those little places.

Being a normally very independent character, Henry gave the same answer that many older people give when offered help, stating there were others who needed the help of the nurses far more than him. Actually at this time he really did need qualify for assistance as he was a very sick man, having been seriously injured in a farm accident. His strength and confidence over came any feelings of self pity, he hated being bed ridden and pampered by others. This was not an opinion shared by all patients, some of us loved the attention of young nurses in what ever shape or form, and I was no exception. But like many red blooded male patients, my interest in the young nurses was purely randy, as long as the wife was not around!

The attention sought from doctors and nurses is not always governed by bodily reactions, some more unfortunate people desperately seek any form of attention to fill the aching gaps in their lives. Often the lonely or unhappy patients attempt to prolong their stay in hospital by pretending to be in a worse state of health than they actually were. Some because they enjoyed the sensation of being cared for, others just to have company and someone to talk to as they lived alone, habitually not seeing or speaking to anyone for days at a time. These patients are easy to identify, moving freely about the ward and cheerfully chatting to other patients, until a doctor appeared in the ward. Then they were suddenly struck down with the inability to get out of bed, no appetite and all sorts of mysterious aches and pains appeared. Henry was not one of these! His greatest wish was to return home to his farm and continue his life. Being an invalid was not for Henry.

Henry was located in the bed next to mine, I did not take much noticed of him at first, I was also very ill myself and could not be bothered to listen to, or attempt to understand the conversations that flittered round the room. The first time he caught my attention came one

194

morning when an improvement in my condition allowed me to sit up in bed and take note of my surroundings. I was fully familiar with the ward and its layout as I had been there many times. I did not need to accustom myself to where I was, or where the toilet could be found or even how to escape if I needed to! I already knew all this, especially how to escape, so it was to my fellow patients that my attention was drawn. Nothing of the ordinary here either, mostly old men coughing, farting and grunting as they festered in their beds awaiting the next hot drink or meal time to brighten their day.

Suddenly the curtain dividing my bed space from my neighbour was rapidly dragged aside and the chap in a bed next to mine peered at me across my bedside cabinet. It was Henry.

'You alright mate?' enquired Henry in his gruff voice.

'Yeah I think so,' I replied.

'Good,' continued Henry, 'I don't want anyone snuffing it next to me!'

'Cheers! Nice to know you care.'

'Didn't mean it like that mate, just nice to see ee feeling better.'

'Thanks.'

'Don't mention it.'

And that was it! The curtains were adjusted back to their original position and I was alone once more as I gently returned to my unconscious state.

Some time later I was rudely awoken by the sound of loud talking coming from somewhere close. Forcing open my bleary eyes I discovered a huge mobile X-ray machine held tightly in the grasp of a young male radiographer, standing uncertainly at the foot of Henry's bed. The radiographer had obviously arrived to take an X-ray of Henry's chest, and Henry was not too happy about the situation!

'What do you think you're gonna do with that bleddy contraption?' asked an irate Henry.

'It's OK sir, I just need to take a picture of your chest for the doctor,' replied the now nervous young man.

'Why?'

'Because your doctor has requested an X-ray.'

'Why?'

'I expect he needs to see if you are getting better. It's quite normal and won't hurt. It'll only take a minute.'

'Why does ee, who ever the bugger is, need a picture of me insides to see if I'm better? Let the lazy sod come see for 'imself. Suppose he'll want me holiday snaps next. I don't need anymore bleddy prodding and messing around!'

'It is simply so doctor can check on your condition,' sighed the young man.

'Hey, isn't that the stuff that can affect yer privates?' exclaimed Henry suddenly.

'Excuse me?'

'You know, those ray thingies are supposed to stop ee having kids, that right?'

'Er. Well yes, that's why I wear this lead lined apron. But it won't affect you sir.'

'What do ee mean, won't affect me? I'm not a bleddy eunuch!'

'One x-ray is not harmful; I wear the apron because I'm taking X-rays all day and every day. There is no harm to you sir.'

'Bugger that,' said Henry 'What if I decide to have more kids?'

The thought of Henry fathering more children at his age filled me with mental pictures I did not want. I also pondered the conception that Henry considered himself still capable of bringing more children into the world. And what his wife may say if he dared even suggest it! I could see many of the other patients were following this farce as much as I, several were grinning quite broadly while listening to the exchange.

'I promise you sir, this will not harm you.'

'You got a spare apron on that thing?'

'Yes sir. We always carry an extra one in case a doctor or nurse cannot leave the patient's side while they have an X-ray. Why?'

'Well pass the damn thing over `ere then.'

'Pardon sir?'

'I said pass that lead pinny over `ere.'

'Why sir?'

'I'll put the thing over me bollocks then ee can take as many bleddy pictures as ee like!'

'I don't think I'm allowed to do that sir.'

'Well ee can bugger off then. I ain't having no rays messing up me bollocks for no one! Take it or leave it,' announced a very stubborn looking Henry.

Henry won the battle. With a sigh of resignation the radiographer gently laid the spare lead lined apron across Henry's lap before proceeding to take an X-ray of Henry's chest. First Henry was asked to sit up while the X-ray plate was positioned behind his back.

'Bleddy hell, that's cold,' cried Henry, 'ee trying to give me a heart attack on top of everything else son?'

'Sorry sir, please lie back against the plate as straight as you can. Don't worry, it'll soon warm,' replied the very cautious young man.

'Bleddy hope so,' Henry retorted.

The radiographer completed his task with as much haste as the procedure would allow, fending off curses and unfavourable comments from Henry as he did so. All finished he wheeled the X-ray machine rapidly from the room, leaving Henry to straighten his bed clothes and manoeuvre into a comfortable position again.

'So, you hoping for more kids Henry?' asked one of the patients with a smile.

'Not bleddy likely!' replied Henry, 'I just wanted to stir up that cocky young sod. That damn pinny thing was bloody heavy, dunno about protecting me bollocks, that thing nearly crushed `em!'

The entertainment persisted over the next few days as Henry's health improved, allowing him to continue his antics in various ways with almost all who dared to enter our ward. From nurses being sent running red faced and giggling to doctors both junior and senior having their expertise questioned and refuted whenever they tried to examine him. Confusion reigned as one incident concerning a young male nurse nearly caused both Henry and I some serious trouble, mainly due to Henry's idea of a whisper actually resembling a fog horn at full volume!

One of the other patient's on the ward was receiving specialist care. The patient called Derek had a rare illness and required the knowledge of a small team of experts, a typical NHS team consisting of one doctor! Though he was expected to make a full recovery it was still necessary for him to receive specific treatment to ensure a cure. He was one of the lucky ones whose condition had been discovered early enough to be successfully treated and his discharge from hospital was eminent. The dedicated doctor had been put in charge of Derek's aftercare, which is the facility offered by specialist nurses, dieticians and local community assistance that would provide continuing care at home following discharge. The consultant doctor was tall, slim, smartly dressed, and quite obviously gay! He flounced into the ward each day with a wiggle of hips and an airy, slightly superior attitude. Always immaculately attired in the latest fashion suitable for his position within the hospital and his status in authority, he made the other doctors appear scruffy. Which in truth several of them were. Derek did not mind that his doctor seemed rather effeminate; in fact the doctor could have been a raving transvestite, or even a politician for all he cared! Derek was simply grateful for the help he was receiving and was very impressed with the concern and empathy shown by the doctor assigned to his care. We could all see that the doctor was gay but we also noted he was working hard to ensure Derek had the best possible treatment. The obvious sexual inclination of Derek's doctor was observed and accepted by all but as yet had not been noticed by Henry, yet.

Awareness arrived one morning while Mike the male nurse was making beds and ensuring we had all toileted, washed or showered and helped to shave those who could not manage the task themselves. Mike was a great guy, very knowledgeable and extremely helpful to both staff and patients alike. Though not tall, Mike possessed a good physique making him definitely capable in all manual aspects of his job and was liked by all. That day Mike was busy making the bed belonging to a patient in the bed next to Derek when the specialist doctor minced into the ward. No one was talking at that time of the morning; we were all still shell shocked from the ridiculously early morning starts favoured by the night staff in hospitals. Breakfast and ablutions completed, we had all settled down for a lazy, boring morning; expecting to be bothered only by the odd doctor, phlebotomist or physiotherapist marching in to administer their particular brand of attention to a patient or victim, depending on how one viewed this ritual punishment.

The doctor first spoke to Derek, enquiring as to his condition this morning and checking his medical notes before drawing the curtains round Derek's bed in order to examine him in privacy. The examination did not take long and the curtains were duly reopened to expose both to the ward again. A few more spoken words between them before the doctor minced out of the ward once more. Nurse Mike had completed making the bed and was straightening to move on to the next bed as the doctor exited the ward. Regrettably on this occasion Henry noticed him as he passed through our ward towards the doors. Henry then looked across at me with an enlightened expression on his square face. Seconds passed before Henry spoke in his normal high decibel whisper.

'Hey, is `ee queer?' he enquired.

'Shhhh!' I quickly attempted to halt what I knew was to come.

'Well `ee looks like one of them. D'you reckon `ee's queer then?'

Before I could answer, nurse Mike had looked up in shock at both Henry and I, his eyes held an angry accusation as he turned to face us.

'What did you say?' he asked.

'Nothing Mike,' I replied.

'It wasn't nothing! I heard you say something. What did you say?'

Again I tried to pacify him by appearing unconcerned as I answered, 'It was nothing, just Henry making a comment. Honest!'

'I'm not bloody gay! I heard you,' he insisted through clenched teeth, 'How dare you say that about me? I'm purely hetero I'll have you know. How dare you! What makes you say I'm bloody gay? I suppose it's because I'm a nurse, isn't it?'

Henry stared back at him in silence with a complete lack of understanding at what had happened. As I realised what had occurred I could barely hold back the laughter but I managed, just! Any indication of merriment certainly would not have been appropriate at that time. Mike marched over and positioned himself between mine and Henry's beds and stood glaring first at Henry than at me.

'Who the hell do you think you are? Making accusations like that? You can't say things like that, that's how rumours start!' Mike almost shouted.

'What ee on 'bout?' enquired a puzzled Henry to the angry and insulted Mike standing before him.

I had never, ever seen Mike so angry and offended, he was normally a placid and pleasant young man, but between Mike's obvious pain at being, as he thought, insulted. To Henry's total lack of understanding regarding the situation unfolding in front of me. Then the penny dropped. I had forgotten that Henry's hearing was not good, in fact he suffered from a common complaint of those entering their senior years, and in Henry's case, no doubt from working round noisy farm machinery for much of his life. It was his lack of hearing that caused Henry to whisper as quietly as a jet aeroplane. And it was apparent he had no idea why Mike was so upset with him. Quickly I spoke up in an attempt to both calm the situation and explain Henry's comments.

'No, no Mike. He wasn't talking about you! He was referring to Derek's doctor, not you. Sorry Derek,' I finished with a wry smile at Derek.

'That's OK,' said Derek, 'I had noticed that fact myself but don't care because he seems a good doctor and I'm sure he is doing his best for me.'

Mike was still staring at both me and Henry, unsure if my explanation really encompassed Henry's original reason for his outburst. Henry was looking sheepish and confused, not totally sure what he had done, his lack of full hearing meant he had failed to understand that as the doctor had just left the room, Mike had assumed his comments were directed at him.

'Sorry Mike,' I continued, 'Henry has only just figured out that the doctor treating Derek is not quite of a heterosexual persuasion. He was not aiming his comment at you, we all know how red blooded you are, we've seen you with the nurses!'

'Oh bleddy `ell!' exclaimed Henry as realisation hit him, 'hey I'm sorry mate, I didn't mean ee, honest, but surely ee've seen that doctor? He's gotta be queer ain't he? Walking round like that, not trying to hide it is `ee?'

At that very moment the doctor in question re-entered the ward to collect some forgotten medical notes from the foot of Derek's bed. With a smile at Derek, and a sly interested glance at Mike, he left the room once more. At once all the tension created by the misunderstanding evaporated as unrestrained mirth broke out amongst the patients, and poor Mike saw for himself what had caused Henry's outburst.

'Ahh ok,' answered a relived Mike, happy now that his sexuality was not in question.

'But you still can't say things like that Henry. He's a fully qualified doctor, it doesn't matter which way he leans. You've really got be more careful in what you say, suppose he'd heard you and made a complaint?'

'Yeah, sorry. I didn't think. It caught me by surprise seeing a queer wandering round a men's ward in hospital,' muttered an abashed Henry.

'Bloody hell mate, you can't say things like queer these days either. Everyone is entitled to follow their own lives and just because he's a doctor and gay, it doesn't mean you're in any risk. I don't think he'd fancy you anyway!'

'Why not?' enquired an indignant Henry.

'You're not his type. You're too old, too knackered and too bloody ugly!'

This last statement was spoken with a huge grin as Mike began to see the lighter side of the exchange, and the absolutely un-politically correct opinions of an old farmer.

'You're also not supposed to call them queer anymore. People who are attracted to the same sex are not to be discriminated against; it's not allowed to call them queers, or bent or queens. The title is gay, I believe.' said Mike while desperately trying to keep a poker face.

'Can't see why not,' said Henry, 'people called things as they saw em in my day. All this bleddy pussy footing around in case some sod gets upset is bleddy daft. Ee seems a good doctor though, and I'm sorry ee thought I was talking about you.'

'Yes well you've got to learn not to open your mouth before your brains engaged Henry; you can get into a lot of trouble these days. I'm not gay and he is and so what? I have gay friends, that's how I know they prefer the title *gay* rather then some of the derogatory comments you were making.'

'Huh! I remember when gay jus' meant happy! That's buggered now.'

'True, but we are both here to make sure you and all the other patients are cared for and leave hospital recovered and well. So please keep your dodgy comments to yourself Henry, before we both get into trouble.'

After these words of advice Mike left the room, smiling broadly now and eager to pass on what had occurred to his colleagues. Henry was still muttering, not totally convinced he had said anything wrong. His world was in pure black and white, not being able to say out loud what he thought seemed unfair to Henry. In his opinion the doctor was queer and should not be offended by being described as such. After all he had been called an old git or miserable bugger plus countless other choice names many times in his life and he did not take offence. Though he had once belted a guy who had insulted his favourite cow!

The events of this morning continued to reduce the boredom of the ward throughout that day and the next. Whenever poor Mike came into our ward, any patient up and about would deliberately begin mincing around. Others when speaking to Mike kept calling him a *'Dear boy'* or *'Sweetie'* plus an assortment of other references that hinted that Mike's sexuality were not quite as straight as he pertained. Mike realised he had made himself the butt of these jokes but took it all in good humour; he knew each of us would eventually be discharged, and peace would reign once more.

Henry continually proved to be a very engaging patient, he habitually managed to cause uproar and confusion amongst both patients and the unfortunate staff rotated to care for us. His light hearted wit and amusing slant on modern life was a refreshing distraction from our aches, ails and pains, he made our hospital internment bearable.

The next episode involved Henry demonstrating his own style of domestic and communication skills. He failed. It was evening visiting time and most of the beds where surrounded by friends and relatives, all attempting to maintain a cheerful conversation with the victim trapped amidst them in a hospital bed. The volume had reached its peak as everyone had found the correct decibel level for them to be heard in their immediate surroundings. No one was taking any notice of fellow patients or their visitors; the concentration of each small group was focused on the reason for their visit to this medical circus. The staring stage that all visitors go through was long over. The *staring stage* is the period when new visitors to the ward spend much of their time peering at the other patients in interest, trying to mentally diagnose each one and secretly praying that what ever it is was not contagious! As our little group of wayward patients had been together for some days with no newcomers, all that needed to be seen, pondered on, discussed or marvelled at had been achieved. No new distractions or entertainment was likely at this stage.

I had noticed that Henry's wife was absent this evening, instead a gentleman around the same age as Henry appeared, somewhat uncertainly beside Henry's bed. As both men were of the more mature age and as it became evident, both were farmers, their volume of conversation quickly climbed above the existing capacity settled at by all others in the ward. The decibel level and content of the new conversation between the two farmers gradually gained our interest, and attention was drawn to the two as they began a task that was obviously very alien to each of them.

Henry decided it was time for him to get back into bed for the night. He had been allowed up and about recently as his health had improved sufficiently and he was able to move around once more. His movements were still slow and often painful but he managed to walk to the toilets and shuffle around the ward. This delighted Henry as he was not a person who enjoyed laying about not doing anything; he was usually a very active man. However getting back into bed proved a problem, Henry was not yet fully capable of fully manoeuvring his injured body but was reluctant to call for a nurse. And besides, his friend Sid who had come to visit this evening offered to help, without realising what was actually required of him.

Henry stood up from his chair beside his bed and began to strip off his shirt; Sid manfully stepped in to assist.

'Slow down Henry; I'll give ee a hand,' said Sid as he moved towards Henry and grasped his shirt.

'Cheers mate,' grunted Henry as he struggled with the garment. 'I gotta put that jammy jacket on next.'

'OK; `ere it `tis.'

'Right; can ee undo me belt? Tis a bit tight and I ain't got the strength in me.'

'I can't go fiddling with yer belt mate! What er people gonna think?'

'Don't you worry `bout them other buggers,' said Henry, 'I can't do it meself so ee gotta help.'

'Bleddy well keep ee still then, `tis hard enough as it is, never had to mess with someone else's belt before. There; that's got un.'

'Didn't the missus ever wear a belt when ee was courting then?' asked Henry with a small grin.

'Nah; she always wore skirt, she never liked to `ang around!'

Henry's belt undone, he dropped his trousers and stepped out of them.

'I ain't taking yer pants off. Bugger that!' exclaimed Sid.

'Oh don't fuss, I gonna keep me draws on. Bleddy jammy's gape too much in the front. Don't wanna scare those pretty young nurses do I?'

Sighing with relief, Sid picked up the pyjama bottoms from the bed and handed them to Henry, who looked back at Sid with an expression of resignation.

'Well gimme a bleddy `and then. I can't pull those flammin' things up by meself!'

'Well you jus' make sure every things tucked in properly. Don't want to lose me eyes!' retorted Sid.

Henry finally managed to get his pyjama bottoms on and secured, Sid was not much help at all as he stood back as quickly as possible once he had gotten the pyjama trousers above Henry's knees. It was very evident that Henry was not a shy person. All this activity was conducted without drawing the curtains round for privacy. Most of the other visitors had stopped their conversations and stared in amazement at the two old farmers. My wife who had managed the long train journey in to see me was growing very red in the face as she tried hard not to laugh out loud at the scene playing out right beside her at the next bed.

Once Henry was decently covered with his bed attire, his gaze moved towards his bed, a thoughtful frown wrinkling his forehead as he considered the next problem. Carefully and slowly he sat on the side of his bed. He next gently kicked off his slippers and attempted to swing his legs up onto the bed, but with no avail, his injuries were still too painful to allow such an energetic exercise.

'Grab me feet and swing em up onto the bed will ee Sid?' he asked, 'Whoa! Not that bleddy fast! Gimme body time to move round with em. Slo-wly like.'

'Sorry,' said Sid, 'you didn't say nought about slowly. I ain't a mind reader ee knows.'

'Tis a bugger! Can't even get me feet up, can't do much damn work like this,' replied Henry with a grimace. 'I'm like a bleddy old man `ere.'

'Well ee are a bleddy old man.'

'Not that bleddy old I ain't! I could still drive that knackered tractor and chuck cow shit before I came `ere. Can't do it now.'

'Ahh don't fret, ee'll soon be up and about again. You gotta get better first, no use runnin' before ee can walk again.'

'Run! Run? Are you damn mad? I can't run! Can't even get me feet off the floor so how the hell am I gonna run anywhere?'

'Come on, you know what I mean, just take it steady till you're better, that's all.'

'Yeah I know,' said Henry sadly, 'Tis takin' so bleddy long, that's the trouble. Feel so damn useless.'

'Don't ee fret,' soothed Sid, 'ee'll be sorted soon. Now what ee want me to do 'bout this `ere bed? Tis `lectric ain't it?'

'Suppose so, it's got wires dangling and buttons on that thing over there, so must be `lectric.'

Henry was now lying on his bed but obviously he was not comfortable. The new hospital beds can be folded into almost any position required by the patient, and Henry's had been set previously by a nurse in the sitting up arrangement. The top third of the bed had been raised to allow Henry to lay on his back in an up right posture; but this was not how he wanted to sleep. Plus one of his pillows had been placed at the foot of his bed to support his feet and his blanket was folded tightly across the bottom of the bed to maintain some form of tidiness during the day. Many patients, including myself hate being in bed all day and so tended to use the armchair allocated beside our bed. Others feel more comfortable lying on their beds throughout the day and of course there were those who were mobility infirmed and had to stay in bed.

'I gotta lay down, can ee put this back bit down?' Henry asked Sid.

'How'd I do that?'

'Use that 'lectric thing down there.'

'Down where?'

''Tis hanging over the bottom of the bed there, just there. See it? Ee looks like one of those TV remote things,' said Henry pointing to a small control handset positioned over the foot board of his bed.

'What button do I press then?' said Sid.

'I dunno. Jus have a look at the bugger and see what it says.'

'It don't say naught, jus pictures.'

'Well look fur a picture that shows this 'ere top bit 'o me bed then!'

'This it?'

'No; no! That's lifting flamin' me feet. Other end. Don't wanna sleep arse over tit. Bleddy 'ell!'

'Oh sorry, what about this un then?'

'No that's not bleddy right. Now me arse is lifting. Try another un.'

'I'm trying me best, 'tis confusing this new fangled thing. How 'bout this un?'

'Whoa! What you doing now?' cried Henry as his whole bed began to rise up.

'Oh hell, 'tis complicated, never ee mind, I'll have a stab at this un.'

'Yep that's un, lower it slowly. Right 'o, that's better, didn't want to be stuck sat up all night staring at that miserable bugger over there.'

Henry indicated to the patient immediately opposite. The non-offended patient made an indication of his own, raising two fingers in response.

'So what ee want now?'

'Pass us that cushion down there Sid,' asked Henry pointing at the pillow resting at his feet.

'What cushion? Ain't no cushions 'ere. You got *Mad Cow Disease* now Henry?'

'That bleddy cushion there, 'tis right beside you. Heave un up here will ee?'

'Ah you mean the pillow, why didn't ee say so?'

'I did say so! Cushion, pillow, what's the bleddy difference?'

'Well a cushion is fur chairs, pillows is fur beds,' explained Sid patiently.

'Don't ee try being funny Sid; jus chuck the damn thing up 'ere. Ta. I need the *pillow* under me head, not me feet.'

'There! Snug as a bug. So what else ee want me to do? Never been a nurse before, don't think I fancy it anyhow, too many old farts moaning 'bout cushions.'

Henry was now lying flat on the bed with his pillows correctly positioned behind his head. Sid looked slightly flustered at all the help he was being asked to give. As a farmer he was quite used to nursing animals, often remaining awake through the night to care for lambing sheep or a cow that was about to calf. But undertaking such tasks for a fellow human being was almost beyond his comprehension and his deeply ingrained sense of decency. Not only was the hospital environment disconcertingly alien to him, but seeing his old friend so vulnerable and helpless was causing his mind to rebel against such strange events. Panic was being to rise inside the hapless Sid.

'Well ee can lower me bleddy bed again Sid, I'm getting vertigo up 'ere! Jus find the button on that 'lectric thing like ee did before . . . . Arrggh! What the hell you doing?'

Henry's bed had shot rapidly down, virtually causing Henry to bounce into the air. Sid had unwittingly pressed the button that instantly lowers and levels the bed in emergencies such as cardiac arrest or other serious conditions that requires immediate access to the patient by the doctors and nurses.

'Sorry,' said Sid unabashed, 'Well you're down again anyway so it don't matter.'

'What ee mean; don't matter? I thought I was in a bleddy car crash! Didn't know anything in this 'ere hospital could move so fast!'

'Yeah OK, don't ee make such a fuss! So you all done now?'

'How the hell am I done now? I'm lying like a bleddy stiff on this bleddy bed. I gotta get in it now so I need that there cover pulled up. Can ee do it Sid?'

'Oh that I can do,' said Sid as he reached with all the tender care a rough handed farmer can give.

'Whoa! Stop! Sid, what ee doing?'

'I'm trying to get this damn sheet out from under yer feet. That's all. What's up with ee now?'

'I'm bleddy sore 'ere you know. You can't yank me feet up in the air like that. You nearly pulled the buggers off! If ee gotta lift me feet, do it slowly and GENTLY!' Henry finished with a bellow.

'Okay, okay. No need to get all et up 'bout it! Yer feet are still there; hang on while I get the covers out from under.'

'Oww! Buggerit! Careful!'

'Stop whining, 'tis done now.'

'Thank fu . . . . Christ for that.'

'Right 'o, how far up you want these covers? Up over yer head?' sniggered Sid.

'Don't be daft, I ain't dead yet. Jus reach em up to me and I'll sort un. Thanks.'

'Phew!' sighed Sid, 'If you were a cow I'd put ee down. All that bleddy fuss. Anyway, you sorted now?'

'Yeah, thanks Sid. I just gotta . . . oww! Bleddy hell! Oww!'

'What's up now mate?' asked Sid quickly as his friends face turned red and he began squirming under the bed sheets.

'It's me . . . oww! I've got me . . . fugging hell! Me jammy's have slid up tight between me arse cheeks and are cutting off me bollocks! Help!'

'Sorry Henry, I ain't digging em out for ee! Bugger that!'

Still squirming Henry shouted, 'Pull those bleddy covers off me, now!'

Sid quickly obliged. 'Tis done mate.'

'Arrghh, Buggerit! Pull me jammy's down a bit! Hurry before I loose me knackers!'

'What? I ain't going pull yer jammy's off, I only just put the buggers on!'

'Pull em!' shouted Henry.

'Okay, okay! Stop hollering. There 'tis done.'

Sid pulled the offending pyjama bottoms down a few inches, not willingly to risk his masculinity by dragging them down further.

'Ahhh, that's better. Tis okay I've sorted em. Me bleddy jammy bottoms had slid up me arse so tight they were cutting me in 'alf! Give us me covers again please Sid,' sighed Henry.

'You sure?'

'Yeah, all fine now, that'll do fur the night I 'ope. Thanks Sid.'

Henry shuffled carefully under his bed covers and made himself comfortable while Sid watched in relief that his friend no longer needed his assistance. As Henry rearranged his bedside table and sipped at a drink, Sid quietly put on his coat. Peace returned.

'Right Henry, I gotta go, 'tis time for milking. Get yerself well,' said Sid as he turned towards the door. 'Will try see ee again soon, but not at bleddy bed time!'

'Okay. Thanks a lot Sid, would 'ave been buggered if ee weren't 'ere.'

'Course ee wouldn't have mate, that's what them pretty lil nurses is fur. Anyways, you get yerself better and ee'll be back throwing manure at the postman again in no time. Yer missus will be in ta see ee tomorra, so take it steady and I'll see ee agin.'

As Sid left the ward he called 'Night Henry.'

'Night Sid.'

'Night John boy,' came a mutter from one of the patients.

Henry did make a full recovery and eventually was discharged home to his beloved farm, much to the disappointment of his fellow patients.

I have continued to make regular trips into hospital and I will probably do so in the future. So who knows, there may be more telling of stories and tall tales in the offering, as I once again enjoy the pleasures of today's marvellous, modern medicinal science and establishments.

Printed in Great Britain
by Amazon.co.uk, Ltd.,
Marston Gate.